Making the Grade

Making the Grade

Promoting Positive Outcomes for Students with Learning Disabilities

Nicholas D. Young
Kristen Bonanno-Sotiropoulos
Jennifer A. Smolinski

ROWMAN & LITTLEFIELD
Lanham • Boulder • New York • London

Published by Rowman & Littlefield
An imprint of The Rowman & Littlefield Publishing Group, Inc.
4501 Forbes Boulevard, Suite 200, Lanham, Maryland 20706
www.rowman.com

Unit A, Whitacre Mews, 26-34 Stannary Street, London SE11 4AB

British Library Cataloguing in Publication Information Available

Library of Congress Cataloging-in-Publication Data Available

ISBN 9781475841930 (hardback: alk. paper) | ISBN 9781475841947 (pbk. : alk. paper) | ISBN 9781475841954 (electronic)

∞ ™ The paper used in this publication meets the minimum requirements of American National Standard for Information Sciences Permanence of Paper for Printed Library Materials, ANSI/NISO Z39.48-1992.

Printed in the United States of America

Nicholas D. Young

With great humility, I dedicate my contributions to this book to my uncle, Robert O. Young, who at the age of 92, is a role model for how to live life to the fullest. Uncle Robert is a WWII veteran who served in the U.S. Navy (1942-1948) before switching branches to complete his distinguished military career in the U.S. Air Force (1949–1969). Among his many interesting assignments, Uncle Robert served on the U.S. Navy's first aircraft carrier, the USS *Langley*, for a short period as part of its initial commissioning before transferring for a longer stint on the USS *Humboldt*. While on the *Humboldt*, as part of D-Day preparations, his vessel recovered naval personnel who were on a sinking ship hit by the Germans; and they towed the captured German U-boat *505* to shore, which is now the only submarine of its kind on display in the United States (as part of an exhibit in the Museum of Science and Industry in Chicago, Illinois). On a more personal level, Uncle Robert, as the oldest of twelve children of his generation, always took a personal interest in each of the members of the large Young family; and I publicly thank him for letting me win at checkers and spending time talking with me about our mutual interest in poultry when I was young. He continues to be one of the few people in my life who knows anything about the New Jersey Giant chickens I have in my backyard. For his honorable service, and living a life committed to family and friends, I want the readers of this book to admire my Uncle Robert as much as I do.

Kristen Bonanno-Sotiropoulos

I would like to take this opportunity to dedicate my portion of this book to my father, Thomas Bonanno. Dad - you have shown me what hardwork and dedication can help you achieve in life. Even though I didn't understand when I was little that you were simply trying to teach me how to grow up to be a strong and self-sufficient woman, I do now. I can't thank you enough for the love, guidance, and support you have and continually show to me on a daily basis. Your belief in me and my abilities gives me the courage to achieve my goals and dreams. You are my strength, wisdom, and my hero.

Jennifer Smolinski

With pride and gratefulness, I would like to dedicate my portion of this book to my family, Chad, Hannah, Ben, and Ryan. Not only did they have much more patience with the writing process than I did, they took care of the world around me. If it was not for their love and support this project would not have been possible.

Contents

Preface

Making the Grade: Promoting Positive Outcomes for Students with Learning Disabilities is an informative primer for educators (including special education and general education teachers), school administrators, parents, and other service providers, who, armed with the knowledge of best practices across all domains, become better advocates and interventionists for struggling students. While their general education peers naturally access academics, make social connections, and regulate their emotions, students with learning disabilities may not be as fortunate and often benefit from specific strategies and interventions to improve outcomes.

The unique characteristics of students with learning disabilities are but one piece of a much larger puzzle considered in this tome. The requirements under federal law as they pertain to special education in general, and students with disabilities specifically, include identification and use of evidence-based interventions during both the pre-referral process and after, examples of supports for meeting the needs of this population, and the importance of teacher knowledge in supporting the teaching and learning process.

Designed to be a valuable resource, this book provides educators, administrators, practitioners, and families with a clear understanding of how to meet the instructional, emotional, and social needs of students with learning disabilities. Readers will benefit from the extensive research provided and will gain an appreciation for the importance of collaboration, creating safe and supportive learning environments, and effectively implementing interventions.

The motivation for writing this book comes from several concerns:

- *Our belief that creating learning environments that incorporate collaboration and acceptance of all students is essential for students with learning disabilities;*
- *Our knowledge that approximately 42 percent of children receiving special education services are identified as having a learning disability (National Center for Learning Disabilities, 2014; US Department of Education, 2014);*
- *Our awareness that students with learning disabilities can achieve positive outcomes through consistent and effective teaching strategies;*
- *Our commitment to ensuring that all students experience positive academic, emotional, behavioral, social, and independence gains; and*
- *Our confidence that partnering with families, practitioners, educators, and peers best supports all students in the quest for positive outcomes.*

Each chapter describes and explains the many facets necessary for student success. Chapter 1 provides an overview of students with learning disabilities and delineates the most common disabilities. Also described are district and educator roles and responsibilities according to federal law.

Advocacy and collaboration are the cornerstones of student success, especially for those with learning disabilities. Chapter 2 takes a closer look at how schools and families can partner to provide valuable support systems and offers the reader a better understanding of procedural safeguards meant to protect students.

Chapter 3 carefully examines the prereferral process. This includes a detailed look at Response to Intervention (RTI) as a multilevel support system that can be used to identify struggling students so that appropriate research-based interventions can be put into place quickly instead of waiting for students to fall behind.

Exposing the reader to the importance of the Individualized Education Plan/Program (IEP), chapter 4 offers a breakdown and a thorough explanation of each critical federally required component. In addition, the writing of IEP goals is discussed in depth and the reader is provided with concrete examples of well-written objectives. Finally, the chapter includes alarming outcome statistics of students with disabilities that further highlight the need for effective programming.

Among many related challenges, research has shown that students with learning disabilities exhibit a higher rate of anxiety and depression. For this reason, chapter 5 focuses on social-emotional learning, which emphasizes the creation of a safe learning environment for all students. When educators are armed with this knowledge, they are better able to embed social-emotional instructional practices, strategies, and tools into their classrooms, and as a result, all students will learn techniques to help self-regulate behaviors.

Chapter 6 takes an in-depth look at evidence-based instructional strategies that can be used across all content areas, grade levels, and tiers of RTI. Research continues to support the use of these strategies due to their promising outcomes; however, teacher training is necessary to ensure they are used with fidelity as a way to close the achievement gap.

The benefits of Universal Design for Learning (UDL) and assistive technology options for students with exceptionalities are the foci of chapter 7, which includes excellent examples of free UDL resources and alternative funding sources for purchasing assistive technology equipment, and highlights the importance of incorporating both to increase student outcomes.

Paraprofessionals and educators form an important partnership in the education of students with learning disabilities. Chapter 8 delves into the components that ensure a strong teaching team as well as the professional development that prepares paraprofessionals for their important role.

Chapter 9 explores the importance of professional development for educators as a way to foster positive outcomes in students with learning disabilities. Considerations include ensuring that training is relevant and enhances educator knowledge while providing time to model, observe, reflect, and share what they have learned. Primary Learning Communities (PLCs) are also discussed as an exceptional professional development tool.

The final chapter examines the essential nature of transitions from high school to postsecondary insititutions; and the importance of self-advocavy is underscored. Additionally, the chapter considers the role of the insitution in providing appropriate accomodations under individually designed 504 plans.

After reflecting upon the contents of this book, the reader will be left with an enhanced understanding of the unique attributes and needs of students with learning disablities as well as how to plan and implement interventions to achieve positive educational outcomes on their behalf.

Acknowledgment

A special thank you to Sue Clark, who somehow managed to catch the little things no one else saw, making her editorial assistance especially important to the completion of this book. We will be forever grateful to her for these contributions.

Chapter One

Legal Responsibilities and Our Students

A Close Examination of the Laws and the Students They Protect

One of the most profound cases that changed the shape of the nation's educational future was *Brown v. Board of Education* (1954). In *Brown*, the court ruled that to separate similarly aged children based on race or other qualifications where a state is obligated to provide an education is a violation of the right to education that must be made available to everyone on equal terms (US Courts, n.d.). Essentially, children may not be denied the opportunity to receive a basic education and/or the privileges associated with it.

After this landmark decision to desegregate schools, parents of children with disabilities began legal actions against school districts for discrimination based on the schools' previous decisions to exclude and segregate children with disabilities. The 1954 *Brown* decision was just the beginning of myriad legal changes and positive outcomes that paved the way for other laws that would take root in our educational future (US Courts, n.d.).

Since *Brown v. Board of Education* in 1954 (US Courts, n.d.), many laws have been put in place to protect students with disabilities and provide them with the support and resources they need to succeed in an educational setting. The rights of students with disabilities to receive the same educational opportunities as those students without disabilities is recognized by Congress, which stated that disabilities are a natural part of being an individual human being and in no way diminish the inherent right to participate in or contribute to society (US Department of Education, 2004).

Improving educational outcomes for individuals with disabilities, particularly children, is an essential element of the national policy that ensures equality of opportunity, full participation, independent living, and economic self-sufficiency for those individuals (US Department of Education, 2004).

THE ELEMENTARY AND SECONDARY EDUCATION ACT (ESEA)

The Elementary and Secondary Education Act of 1965, the most far-reaching federal legislation affecting education ever passed by the United States Congress, was enacted to combat the achievement gap between low-income, neglected, and homeless families and higher-income families. Provisions within ESEA aim to close the gap by setting benchmarks and goals to measure the progress of students (Virginia Commonwealth University, n.d.).

ESEA established federal funding for primary and secondary school education and set forth a national curriculum. ESEA also provided a national system to hold schools accountable and increase equality in education. Most importantly, Title VI of ESEA extended provisions to children with disabilities (Virginia Commonwealth University, n.d.).

SECTION 504 OF THE REHABILITATION ACT OF 1973

Section 504 is a federal law put in place to protect the rights of individuals with disabilities in programs and activities that receive federal financial assistance from the US Department of Education Rehabilitation Act (1973). In part, the statute provides that an otherwise qualified individual with a disability shall not be excluded from the participation in, be denied the benefits of, or be subjected to discrimination based on the fact that he or she has a disability (United States Access Board, n.d.).

Section 504 also requires recipients of federal funds to provide students with disabilities appropriate educational services designed to meet the individual needs of such students to the same extent as the needs of students without disabilities (United States Access Board, n.d.). To fulfill this obligation, school team members, including special education educators, along with a child's parent create a 504 plan that provides services and changes to the learning environment (Understood, 2017a).

Unlike Individual Education Plans, there is no standard 504 plan, and a 504 plan does not have to be a written document. Plans under Section 504 include specific accommodations, supports, and/or services along with the names of the persons responsible for providing services and ensuring how the plan is implemented. Although it varies by state, 504 plans are generally reviewed each year with a reevaluation occurring every three years or when needed (Understood, 2017a).

THE EDUCATION FOR ALL
HANDICAPPED CHILDREN ACT (EHA)

The Education for All Handicapped Children Act (EHA) of 1975 was written to ensure that special education services were available to children with disabilities. Under this act, public schools were required to provide fair and appropriate services along with equal access to education in the least restrictive environment possible (Wright, 2010).

School districts were required to put in place a dispute system for parents to resolve complaints if they believed their children were not being provided a fair and equal education. Parental remedies included those administrative procedures set forth by the school as well as due process and judicial complaint (Wright, 2010).

INDIVIDUALS WITH DISABILITIES EDUCATION ACT (IDEA)

The EHA was revised and renamed the Individuals with Disabilities Education Act (IDEA) in 1990 to improve upon special education and the services available for children with disabilities. Additional amendments were passed in 1997 and 2004 (when it was renamed the Individuals with Disabilities Education Improvement Act, or IDEIA) to ensure equal access to education (Disabilities, Opportunities, Internetworking, and Technology, 2017b).

Key components of IDEA. IDEA consists of four main parts:

Part A—its purpose and relevant definitions;
Part B—requirements for public school for children age 3 to 21;
Part C—requirements for families with infants and toddlers, birth to age 2; and
Part D—resources and national initiatives to improve special education (Special Education News, 2017).

IDEA also set out procedural safeguards (which we will discuss further in later chapters) and set forth appropriate disciplinary measures for students with disabilities (Special Education News, 2017).

By law, schools were now required to make a free appropriate public education available to children with disabilities and to ensure special education and related services to those children with disabilities. The result was that states and public agencies were mandated to provide early intervention, special education, and related services to more than 6.5 million eligible infants, toddlers, children, and youth with disabilities (IDEA Partnership, n.d.).

IDEA Part B. Part B of IDEA states that all public schools receiving federal funding must supply a free appropriate public education to all students with disabilities, including those students with autism, specific learning disabilities, and speech and language impairment, among others (IDEA Partnership, n.d.; Special Education News, 2017).

IDEA also guarantees a free education tailored to individual needs and delivered in the least restrictive environment (IDEA Partnership, n.d.; National Center for Learning Disabilities, 2014). Not only must education and services for children with disabilities be provided in the least restrictive environment, but children with disabilities should be placed in a typical education setting with nondisabled students when feasible (American Psychiatric Association, 2016; IDEA Partnership, n.d.).

Effective educational systems serving students with disabilities should maintain high academic achievement standards and clear performance goals for children with disabilities that are consistent with the standards and expectations set forth for all students in the educational system (IDEA Partnership, n.d.). Appropriate and effective strategies and methods to ensure students have the opportunity to achieve those standards and goals must be provided (National Activities to Improve Education of Children with Disabilities, 2004).

Each student who qualifies under IDEA must have a legal one-year contract called an Individualized Education Program (IDEA Partnership, n.d.). An IEP must clearly define in objective, measurable terms the school outcomes the child is expected to achieve and contain specific methods to track student progress (National Activities to Improve Education of Children with Disabilities, 2004; Special Education News, 2017).

IDEA also mandates that parent(s) participate in developing a student's IEP and that the school report progress to the student's parent(s) as frequently as it would to the parents of students without IEPs (IDEA Partnership, n.d.).

Students with IEPs requalify for special education services every three years (IDEA Partnership, n.d.). Eligibility is determined by a designated special education team that is charged with reviewing more than one assessment tool (i.e., intelligence test) coupled with an academic achievement test (Special Education News, 2017). IDEA also ensures that the rights of children with disabilities and the parents of those children are protected through guaranteed procedural safeguards such as the right to a timely evaluation (National Center for Learning Disabilities, 2014).

1997 Amendments

Significant changes were made to IDEA in 1997 concerning parentally placed private school students. The amendments now required local educational authorities (LEAs) to consult with private school officials prior to conducting child find activities in those locations (Special Education News, 2017). Child find requires state educational agencies (SEAs) and LEAs to locate, identify, and evaluate all children residing in the state who are suspected of having a disability under Part B of IDEA (IDEA Partnership, n.d.; US Department of Education, 2001).

School districts must provide parentally placed in-district private school students with disabilities a genuine opportunity for equitable participation in their special education program. Under the new IDEA, private school students with a disability whom an LEA elects to serve must have a service plan that meets IEP content requirements and is developed, reviewed, and revised consistent with IEP process requirements (US Department of Education, 2001).

The 1997 amendments also provided support initiatives for transition services and required IEPs to include transition plans for identifying appropriate employment and available community resources (US Department of Education, 2010).

2004 Amendments

Enforcement. Federal legislation requires states to develop a plan and to establish and meet targets in the provision of free appropriate education and transition services. Both the 1997 and 2004 amendments to IDEA allowed the federal government to sanction noncompliant states if they failed to meet their educational targets (IDEA Partnership, n.d.).

Transition. In 1997, although schools had to consider transition issues for disabled students, they did not have to set clear goals for a student's life after school. Agencies such as Vocational Rehabilitation, Social Security, and institutions of higher education were not required to participate in transition planning for students (US Department of Education, 2001). With the new 2004 legislation, schools were required to plan for transition by setting clear and concise transition goals and providing transition services (US Department of Education, 2007).

Teachers. State standards for special education teachers were not well defined in 1997, and as a result many special education teachers did not have the skills they needed (US Department of Education, 2001). IDEA 2004 established a standard for highly qualified teachers that required all teachers to be fully certified in special education or pass state special education licensure exams, hold a bachelor's degree, and demonstrate subject knowledge (IDEA Partnership, n.d.).

Accountability. Students with disabilities are included in state and local accountability systems, but in 1997, alternate assessments to measure the progress of students with disabilities did not count (US Department of Education, 2001). As of 2004, alternate assessments are included as part of state and local accountability systems (IDEA Partnership, n.d.).

Funds. Because districts could use 20 percent of any increase in IDEA funds flexibly, for any local purpose, schools often had difficulty serving students with significant disabilities with high-cost needs (US Department of Education, 2001). Due to a change in the law, school districts are now able to use a portion of IDEA funds for educational programs as long as the LEA is in compliance with IDEA (IDEA Partnership, n.d.).

NATIONAL ACTIVITIES TO IMPROVE EDUCATION OF CHILDREN WITH DISABILITIES

The federal government has an ongoing obligation to support activities that contribute to positive outcomes for children with disabilities (National Activities to Improve Education of Children with Disabilities, 2004). Federal funding provides formula and discretionary grants, authorized under IDEA, to assist states and educational service agencies in providing an education for all children with disabilities. These grants support states in special education research to ensure that educators have the necessary tools to improve educational outcomes for children with disabilities (IDEA Partnership, n.d.).

Successes under IDEA

Over the last thirty-five years, more young children with disabilities have received high-quality education, been taught according to the general education curriculum, and learned a wide variety of academic skills (US Department of Education, 2010). Out of these almost 6 million students being served by IDEA Part B, 39.2 percent were students with specific learning disabilities (US Department of Education, 2016).

As a result of the enactment of IDEA (IDEA Partnership, n.d.), in academic year 2013–2014 the number of students with disabilities graduating with a regular diploma was 70.8 percent, and only 18 percent of students with disabilities dropped out of high school without graduating (Horowitz, Rawe, & Whittaker, 2017). Research has also shown that the number of students with disabilities going on to postsecondary undergraduate studies is 6 percent, and of those students 31 percent identified themselves as having specific learning disabilities (Disabilities, Opportunities, Internetworking, and Technology, 2017a).

Future of IDEA

To make progress under IDEA in the future, a strong focus will be needed on strengthening postsecondary transitions and accommodations, juvenile justice, and access to education. Those involved in special education will need to improve upon the 40.7 percent postsecondary completion rate, reduce out-of-school suspensions for children with disabilities, and increase from 2 percent the number of students with disabilities enrolled in advanced classes (American Occupational Therapy Association, 2015; Consortium for Citizens with Disabilities, 2015).

In 2017, $113 million was cut from the funding allocated for the Individuals with Disabilities Education Act. In response, Congress introduced the bipartisan IDEA Full Funding Act, which would increase the federal contribution to IDEA from roughly 15 percent to 40 percent of the costs associated with educating special needs students over the next ten years. On June 15, 2017, the act was referred to the House Committee on Education and the Workforce by the House of Representatives (Litvinov, 2017).

No Child Left Behind Act (NCLB)

The No Child Left Behind Act (NCLB) of 2001 authorized several state-administered federal education programs and reauthorized the Elementary and Secondary Education Act. Under NCLB, states were required to test students in reading and math in third through eighth grade, and again once during high school. The major focus of NCLB was to close student achievement gaps in education by providing all children with a fair, equal, and significant opportunity to obtain a high-quality education. There were four tenets to the bill, including accountability, flexibility, research-based education, and parent options (Klein, 2015).

Accountability seeks to ensure that those students who are disadvantaged, including those with disabilities, achieve academic proficiency. Flexibility allows schools to use federal education funds in a way they deem appropriate to help improve student achievement. Research-based education emphasizes educational programs and practices that have been proven effective through scientific research. Parent options ensure a plethora of opportunities are available for children attending Title I schools (Klein, 2015).

Every Student Succeeds Act (ESSA)

Signed in December 2015, the Every Student Succeeds Act (ESSA) was the next iteration in a long line of educational mandates that began with the Elementary and Secondary Education act of 1965, and replaced NCLB, whose prescriptive requirements had become increasingly more difficult for schools to attain (US Department of Education, 2015a).

ESSA reiterated the goal of fully preparing all students for success in college and future careers and set forth the requirement that educators teach to *all* students the same academic content and maintain high academic standards (US Department of Education, 2015a). With this, teachers now had the room to focus on the students, not just on tests (American Federation of Teachers, n.d.).

The academic standards set by teachers must promote access to the general education curriculum consistent with IDEA, and for those students with disabilities, must be designated in the IEP developed for each student. Student proficiency goals and measures must be clarified and based on grade-level proficiency, and states must use the same definition of grade-level proficiency for all students (Council of Chief State School Officers, 2017).

School accountability. Vital information is now required to be provided to educators, families, and students through statewide assessments that measure students' progress toward those high standards. Schools are accountable for such items as proficiency in reading and math, graduation rates for high schools, English language proficiency, student growth, and at least one other indicator of school quality or success, such as measures of safety, student engagement, or educator engagement (American Federation of Teachers, n.d.).

Under ESSA, there is a continued expectation of accountability and action to effect positive change in those schools that perform at the lowest levels (US Department of Education, 2015a). The lowest-performing 5 percent of schools will no longer be subject to the personnel requirements and punitive sanctions found under NCLB; instead, states will now provide targeted and comprehensive support and improvement through development plans made in conjunction with stakeholders based on all indicators (American Federation of Teachers, n.d.).

Through annual data reporting, important information for parents, teachers, and communities is maintained and provides valuable information about whether all students are achieving, including low-income students, students of color, students with disabilities, and English learners (Senate Committee on Health, Education, Labor & Pensions, 2017).

To help strengthen state and local control, the federal government is prohibited from determining or approving state standards and may not mandate or incentivize states to adopt or maintain any particular set of standards, including the Common Core (Senate Committee on Health, Education, Labor & Pensions, n.d.). States are provided with the opportunity to make reasonable goals and objectives that can be collaboratively established and are in alignment with the needs of students (American Federation of Teachers, n.d.). IEP teams are now poised to make critical decisions regarding students' academic, assessment, and social-emotional needs and can use personalized learning to encourage students to be lifelong learners (Alvarez, 2016).

Assessment tests. Despite a proposal that states should reduce testing that consumes too much instructional time and creates undue stress for educators and students, ESSA still requires states to test at least 95 percent of students, with a higher percentage of students in special education taking the tests

(Kamenetz, 2016). Instead of a federally mandated 100 percent proficiency goal, states now have the responsibility for setting targets and determining how to use federally required tests for accountability purposes (Kamenetz, 2016; Senate Committee on Health, Education, Labor & Pensions, n.d.).

The enactment of ESSA will also help states support educators, with new focus given to developing effective teachers and leaders providing the potential to improve student performance while reducing special education teacher shortages. ESSA has removed the burdensome requirements that all special education teachers be certified in a content area in addition to special education (Senate Committee on Health, Education, Labor & Pensions, n.d.).

Assessment alternatives. Although students with disabilities must be held to the same high achievement standards as students without disabilities, appropriate accommodations must be provided for students with disabilities identified under IDEA. ESSA provides one exception to the use of the same achievement standards for all students. For those students with the most significant cognitive disabilities, states are able to provide alternate assessment measures based on alternative achievement standards, provided these standards are aligned with the challenging state academic content standards. Alternative standards must promote access to the general education curriculum consistent with IDEA and be designated in the IEP for each student, ensuring that a student who meets the alternate academic achievement standards is on track to pursue postsecondary education or employment (Council of Chief State School Officers, 2017).

To enable the inclusion and participation of all students in assessments, states must provide appropriate accommodations, and all assessments must be developed using principles of Universal Design for Learning. By using UDL-appropriate accommodations, including assistive technology where appropriate, barriers to instruction for students with disabilities are reduced while the high achievement expectations for all students are maintained (Council of Chief State School Officers, 2017).

Future of ESSA

Over the last five years, there has been a 34.2 percent increase in the identification of specific learning disabilities (SLD) among school-age children (Horowitz, Rawe, & Whittaker, 2017). Although children with learning disabilities have average or above-average intelligence, there is still a wide achievement gap between them and students without disabilities. Research shows that more than 90 percent of students with SLD scored below proficient on the 2013 National Assessment of Educational Progress (Horowitz, Rawe, & Whittaker, 2017). Despite the demonstrated achievement gap, more than two hundred thousand students entering college in fall 2015 had some type of learning disability (NCES, 2016a).

When schools are unable or fail to provide adequate support for students with disabilities, the associated social, emotional, and behavioral challenges can lead to serious consequences. These consequences can include social isolation, disproportionate disciplinary rates, and an increased likelihood of skipping school, dropping out, and becoming involved with the criminal justice system. For example, students identified with SLD are 31 percent more likely than students without disabilities to experience high levels of being bullied (Horowitz, Rawe, & Whittaker, 2017).

According to the American Psychiatric Association (2016), learning disorders are developmental disorders that begin by school age and involve ongoing problems learning key academic skills such as reading, writing, and math (Silver, 2013). In turn, specific learning disorders are characterized as those that affect individuals who can otherwise demonstrate average abilities essential for thinking or reasoning and interfere with the acquisition and use of academic skills such as oral language, reasoning, written language, and mathematics (*Psychology Today*, 2017; NASET, n.d.).

Diagnosis of Learning Disorders

The diagnosis of a learning disorder is based on a combination of an individual's medical and family history, observation, interviews, history of learning difficulty, school reports, educational and psychological assessments, and standardized tests. Difficulties with learning must not be due to intellectual disabilities, external factors (i.e., economic or environmental), lack of instruction, vision or hearing problems, neurological conditions, or motor disorders (American Psychiatric Association, 2016).

To be diagnosed with a specific learning disorder, a person must have difficulties in at least one of the following areas, with continued symptoms for at least six months despite targeted help: reading, understanding the meaning of what is read, spelling, written expression, understanding number concepts, number facts or calculation, or mathematical reasoning (American Psychiatric Association, 2016; Silver, 2013). Based on these criteria, an estimated 5 to 15 percent of school-age children experience specific learning disorders, with reading disorder (dyslexia) being the most common (American Psychiatric Association, 2016).

DSM-5 diagnostic criteria. The *Diagnostic and Statistical Manual of Mental Disorders*, 5th edition (DSM-5) (Silver, 2013) defines a specific learning disorder as a "neurodevelopmental disorder with a biological origin that is the basis for abnormalities at a cognitive level that are associated with the behavioral signs of the disorder" (p. 68). To be medically diagnosed with a specific learning disorder, an individual must have difficulty learning and using academic skills, demonstrated by at least one of the following symptoms for at least six months despite targeted interventions: inaccurate or slow and effortful word reading; difficulty understanding the meaning of what is read; difficulty with spelling; difficulty with written expression; difficulty mastering number sense, number facts, or calculation; and/or difficulty with mathematical reasoning (Silver, 2013). Learning difficulties should also have begun during a child's school-age years and cannot be better accounted for by intellectual disabilities or mental/neurological disorders (Silver, 2013).

CHARACTERISTICS OF STUDENTS WITH LEARNING DISABILITIES

Children with learning disabilities come from various backgrounds of race, ethnicity, and socioeconomic status and exhibit difficulties in various areas of learning (Horowitz, Rawe, & Whittaker, 2017). In general, students with learning disabilities are of average or above average intelligence with an unseen academic gap between their potential and actual achievement. This is why learning disabilities are often referred to as hidden disabilities (LDA, 2017). It is imperative to remember, though, that hidden disabilities are still disabilities.

There are nine learning and behavioral characteristics of individuals with learning disabilities, including disorders of attention, reading difficulties, poor motor abilities, written language difficulties, oral language difficulties, social skills deficits, psychological process deficits, quantitative disorders, and information processing problems (Lerner, 2000, cited in NASET, n.d.).

Most Common Learning Disabilities within the Classroom

Learning disabilities arise from neurological differences in brain structures and functions, affecting a person's ability to receive, store, process, retrieve, or communicate information (National Center for Learning Disabilities, 2014). The most common types of learning disabilities that occur within a school setting include dyslexia, dyscalculia, dysgraphia, and auditory and language processing disorders.

Dyslexia. Dyslexia is the best-known learning disorder and is often referred to as a language-based disorder. It is characterized by an impediment to the student's ability to read and comprehend text (International Dyslexia Association, 2017a). Students with dyslexia struggle with phonemic awareness and fail to recognize the way words break down according to their sounds. Difficulty can also arise with phonological processing, fluency, spelling, and comprehension. Students with dyslexia also fail to recognize and comprehend the written word, which presents a severe impairment to the ability to read, despite normal intelligence (International Dyslexia Association, 2017a).

Dyscalculia. Dyscalculia is the inability to order numbers. Students diagnosed with dyscalculia often have limited strategies for problem solving as well as trouble performing basic math calculations and/or difficulty with concepts like time, measurement, or estimation (Dyscalculia.org, 2017; Masters in Special Education Program Guide, 2017a). They may also be unable to sort critical extraneous information, recognize the correct computational procedure, or determine whether the answer they obtain is reasonable (Dyscalculia.org, 2017; LDA, 2017).

Dysgraphia. Dysgraphia involves the physical task of writing and difficulty in holding a pencil correctly. It is best exemplified by illegible handwriting (particularly with complex text), inconsistent spacing, poor spatial planning on paper, and difficulty thinking and writing at the same time. Other characteristics include difficulty with written expression, organizing thoughts, redundant writing, or obvious omissions that affect the quality or readability of text (International Dyslexia Association, 2017b). In general, students with dysgraphia struggle with basic sentence structure and grammatical awareness (International Dyslexia Association, 2017b; LDA, 2017; Masters in Special Education Program Guide, 2017).

Auditory processing. Auditory processing disorders adversely affect how sound that travels unimpeded through the ear is processed and interpreted by the student's brain. Students with an auditory processing disorder are not able to recognize subtle differences between sounds in words and have difficulty distinguishing where sounds are coming from (Bellis, 2017). Students also are unable to block out competing background noise, which can make the classroom a very difficult environment for learning (Bellis, 2017; LDA, 2017).

Students who have trouble with auditory processing may also have an additional diagnosis of language processing disorder. Language processing disorders are a specific type of auditory processing disorder in which students have difficulty attaching meaning to sound into groups that form words, sentences, and stories (ASHA, 2014b). More concerning is that these types of disorders can affect expressive language (what someone says to a student) and receptive language (how the student understands what was said) (ASHA, 2014a; LDA, 2017).

Attention-deficit/hyperactivity disorder (ADHD). Attention-deficit/hyperactivity disorder, also commonly known as ADHD, affects more than 6.4 million children (Centers for Disease Control and Prevention, 2017). Students suffering from ADHD have short attention spans, are highly distractible, and have difficulty staying on task, especially in busy, overcrowded classrooms. They are easily distracted and quite often have difficulty in traditional school settings (ASHA, 2014a).

There is an ongoing debate whether ADHD is a true learning disability but there is no question that it is an impediment to learning. Individuals with learning disabilities have measurable deficits in one or more areas of learning and perform at or above average levels in school. Under federal guidelines, ADHD does not meet the definition of a learning disability due to its impact on all areas of learning and cognitive functions rather than any one function alone. A child diagnosed with ADHD who does not have any coexisting learning disabilities is not classified as having a learning disability but as "other health impaired" (Bright Hub Education, 2016).

Children with Learning Disabilities in School Systems

Students identified as having a learning disability account for 42 percent of the 5.7 million students identified as having a disability who receive special education services (Silver, 2013; National Center for Learning Disabilities, 2014). Although this number may seem large, it has actually declined by 18 percent since 2002 (National Center for Learning Disabilities, 2014).

Research suggests that the decline may be due to the expansion of and attention to early childhood education, improvements in reading instruction provided in generalized education, and the dramatic shift in the way learning disabilities are identified. Another factor that may contribute to the decline in numbers is that not all students with learning disabilities actually receive special education (National Center for Learning Disabilities, 2014).

FINAL THOUGHTS

Students with specific learning disabilities are at a disadvantage compared to their peers who do not have learning disabilities. Academic skills associated with the five most common disabilities in the classroom, among other disabilities, continue to be below those expected for the student's age and continue to cause significant interference with educational performance.

In order to offer educational equality and access, many significant laws have been enacted over time that have provided for the protection and enhancement of an education to students with disabilities. Section 504 of the Rehabilitation Act of 1973 guarantees that individuals who are otherwise qualified, despite their disability, shall not be excluded from or denied the benefit of an inclusive learning environment, or be discriminated against because they have a disability.

The Individuals with Disabilities Act sought to improve upon the rights of students to an equal education, providing for the availability of a free public education to disabled students and ensuring they would receive special education services. IDEA also guaranteed an education that was tailored to a student's individual needs in the least restrictive enjoinment.

With the recent enactment of the Every Student Succeeds Act, IDEA was taken one step further and set forth the requirement that educators hold all

8

 Chapter 1

students accountable to the same high academic standards in order to better prepare them for successful careers in postsecondary education and in future employment (US Department of Education, 2015).

POINTS TO REMEMBER

- *As many as 2.3 million students have been identified as having a specific learning disability and receive special education services. Students with disabilities may have accommodations and modifications in order to access the curriculum.*
- *The federal government is obligated to support educational efforts that result in positive outcomes for students with disabilities, and federal grant funding is available to schools in order to support additional programs (*Psychology Today, *2017).*
- *IDEIA and ESSA were enacted to prepare students for success not only in education but in college and future careers. Under these acts, educational systems shall maintain the same high academic achievement standards and clear performance goals for all children.*
- *The five most common learning disabilities in the classroom are dyslexia, dyscalculia, dysgraphia, auditory processing, and ADHD. There is continued debate over whether ADHD is a learning disability or a medical condition, as, unlike learning disabilities, it can be controlled with medication.*
- *Public schools are required to provide equal access to education and special education services in the least restrictive environment for all students. Significant laws have been enacted over the years to support and protect students with disabilities.*

Chapter Two

Advocacy and Collaboration

The Foundation for Student Success

Children are more confident, achieve more, and stay in school longer when parents advocate on their behalf (National PTA, n.d.). It is important that parents become knowledgeable about the rights and protections afforded under the law, particularly the special educational rights and protections under IDEA Part B (IDEA Partnership, n.d.). This federal special education law gives parents a legal right and responsibility to participate in the education of students with disabilities.

Special education services are developed in a decision-making process involving the child's parent(s) and school district staff; thus, procedural safeguards are in place to protect the student's and parents' rights (Pacer Center, 2017). Procedural safeguards are the specific rules that make sure a parent knows what the school district is proposing to do, agrees with the school district's plan, and has a range of opportunities for resolving disagreements with the school district (Massachusetts Department of Education, 2013).

PROCEDURAL SAFEGUARDS TO PROTECT STUDENT AND PARENTAL RIGHTS

Prior Written Notice

Parents can expect to receive a prior written notice after an IEP meeting has been held and a new or annual IEP has been written, or whenever the school district and parents make an evaluation plan for the child, either for the first time or for a reevaluation. School districts must give parents written notice no fewer than fourteen calendar days before the proposed date of an IEP change or the identification, evaluation, refusal, or educational placement, including a free appropriate education, of a student with disabilities (Pacer Center, 2017; Cornell Law School, n.d. i). If the notice includes only a refusal of a request, it must be given to parents within fourteen calendar days of the date the request was made (Pacer Center, 2017).

There is no requirement regarding the way the form should look or be worded and titled, as long as the notice is in writing and covers all the required components (Pacer Center, 2017). The notice must include a clear and specific description of the action the school district proposes or refuses to take and an explanation of the reasons the district is proposing or refusing to take the action. The proposed action should include the specific evaluation procedures and assessments, a list of people by whom they will be done, and records or reports the district used to make their decision (Pacer Center, 2017; US Department of Education, n.d. b).

Any other choices the IEP team considered and the reasons those choices were rejected as well as a description of any additional reasons an action was proposed or refused must be on the prior written notice form. Lastly, a list of resources parents can contact for information on a prior written notice and help understanding Part B of IDEA should be on the form itself (Pacer Center, 2017; US Department of Education, n.d. b).

If a parent objects to a proposal or refusal in the prior written notice, he or she must be given an opportunity for a conciliation conference to try to resolve the disagreement within ten days from the date the district receives the objection. The school district must also inform parents of other alternative dispute resolution procedures such as mediation or facilitated IEP team meetings (Pacer Center, 2017).

Parental Notice and FERPA

Before any major activity to identify, locate, or evaluate children in need, educational agencies must give adequate notice to inform parents about the confidentiality of personally identifiable information. Such information includes a description of the native languages in which the notice may be sent, a description of the children whose personally identifiable information is maintained, the types of information sought, and the methods used to gather such information and how it will be used (Cornell Law School, n.d. h).

Notices must also include a summary of the policies and procedures that agencies must follow regarding storage, disclosure of information to third parties, retention, and destruction of personally identifiable information (Cornell Law School, n.d. h). A description of all the rights of parents and children regarding this information, including the rights under the Family Educational Rights and Privacy Act (FERPA) must also be disclosed (US Department of Education, 2015b).

FERPA applies to schools that receive funding under any program administered by the US Department of Education and gives parents certain rights with respect to their children's education records unless a school is provided with evidence that there is a court order or state law that specifically provides to the contrary. Private and parochial schools at the elementary and secondary levels generally do not receive such funding and are therefore not subject to FERPA (US Department of Education, 2015b).

Under FERPA, a school must provide a parent with an opportunity to inspect and review a student's education records within forty-five days following the receipt of a request. The education record consists of the student's transcript, temporary school record, health records, tests, evaluations, discipline records, and records pertaining to special education eligibility or programs (Massachusetts Department of Education, 2017). A school is required to provide a parent with copies of education records, or make other arrangements, if a failure to do so would effectively prevent the parent from obtaining access to the records (US Department of Education, 2015a).

Parents also have the right to request that inaccurate or misleading information in the student's education records be amended (US Department of Education, 2015a). While FERPA affords parents the right to seek to amend education records that contain inaccurate information, this right cannot be used to challenge a grade, an individual's opinion, or a substantive decision made by a school about a student. The improper disclosure of personally identifiable information derived from education records is prohibited; therefore, information that an educator obtained through personal knowledge, observation, or has heard orally from others, is not protected under FERPA (US Department of Education, 2015a).

One exception to the prior written consent requirement allows school officials to access personally identifiable information in educational records provided the school has a "legitimate educational interest" in the information (US Department of Education, 2015a). "School officials" can include teachers, administrators, staff members, and outsourced institutional services (US Department of Education, 2015a). School officials have a legitimate educational interest if there is a need to review the record to fulfill a professional responsibility (US Department of Education, 2015a).

Another exception permits a school to disclose personally identifiable information from a student's education records, without consent, to another school in which the student seeks or intends to enroll (US Department of Education, 2015a). The improper disclosure of personally identifiable information derived from education records is prohibited; therefore, information that an educator obtained through personal knowledge, observation, or has heard orally from others, is not protected under FERPA (US Department of Education, 2015a).

FERPA rights are afforded to the parent of a student and do not provide for third party rights unless a third party has suffered an alleged violation of their rights under FERPA (US Department of Education, 2015a). A student is considered an "eligible student" when the age of 18 is reached or attends a postsecondary institution. At this time, all rights under FERPA transfer from the parent to the student (US Department of Education, 2015a). A parent of an adult student with a disability will continue to receive all the required notices from the school and will continue to be able to inspect the student's educational records, even if the student makes his or her own educational decisions (Massachusetts Department of Education, 2013).

Consent

Parental consent means that parents have an opportunity and responsibility to agree or disagree with actions a school district proposes or refuses to take (Pacer Center, 2017). According to Part B of the procedural safeguards notice, consent means that a person has been fully informed of all the information associated with a proposed action and that agreement to this action is given voluntarily. Due to its voluntary nature, consent can be withdrawn, in writing, at any point in time, including after a student has begun receiving special education services (Cornell Law School, n.d. b).

Withdrawing consent does not negate any action that may have occurred after consent was granted but before it was revoked. After consent is withdrawn, school districts are not required to change a student's education records to remove any reference to special education (Cornell Law School, n.d. b).

School districts may not conduct an initial evaluation of a student to determine whether the child is eligible for special education services under Part B of IDEA (1990) without first providing the parent(s) with prior written notice and obtaining voluntary consent (Massachusetts Department of Education, 2017; Cornell Law School, n.d. b). Every reasonable effort must be made to obtain informed consent for an initial evaluation to determine if a student has a disability. Consent for an initial evaluation does not mean that consent is also given for the school district to start providing special education services (Cornell Law School, n.d. b; US Department of Education, 2015b).

The parent may refuse consent to one service or activity related to the initial evaluation; however, that cannot be the basis for the school district to deny any other service, benefit, or activity, unless another Part B requirement necessitates such an action (Cornell Law School, n.d. b; US Department of Education, 2015a). If consent is refused, public school districts may, but are not required to, conduct an initial evaluation by using the IDEA's (1990) mediation or due process complaint, resolution meeting, and impartial due process hearing procedures (Cornell Law School, n.d. b; US Department of Education, 2015b).

Schools must also make reasonable efforts to obtain a parent's informed consent before providing special education and related services to a student for the first time (Cornell Law School, n.d. b; US Department of Education, 2015b). If a student is already receiving special education services and is on an IEP, advance written consent is needed to excuse members of the IEP team from a team meeting. If a parent does not agree to excuse the team member, the member must attend the IEP team meeting (Massachusetts Department of Education, 2017).

If a parent fails or refuses to respond to a request to provide consent for services, school districts may not use procedural safeguards such as mediation, due process complaint, resolution meeting, or an impartial due process hearing in order to obtain agreement (Cornell Law School, n.d. b).

Independent Educational Evaluations

Independent educational evaluations (IEE) are conducted by a qualified examiner who is not employed by the school district responsible for the education of the particular student (Massachusetts Department of Education, 2017). An initial evaluation of the student is the first completed assessment to determine whether a disability exists under IDEA (1990) and the nature and extent of special education services provided (Smith, 2004).

Evaluation procedures require that schools use a variety of assessment tools and strategies to gather relevant functional, developmental, and academic information about the child that will help determine whether the student has a disability and the content of the student's IEP. Information related to the student's involvement and progress in the general education curriculum is also included. States must ensure that in evaluating each student with a disability, the evaluation is sufficiently comprehensive to assess the student in all areas and identifies all the student's special needs (Smith, 2004).

Parents have the right to obtain an IEE of a student at public expense if there is disagreement with the school district's initial evaluation. In this situation, the school district is responsible for the burden of proof and must show that the tests completed were appropriate or that the independent evaluation did not meet the school district's criteria. After a hearing, if it is found that the school district's evaluation is appropriate, parents still have the right to an independent educational evaluation, but not at public expense (Cornell Law School, n.d. f).

Current IDEA regulations specify that the right of a parent to obtain an IEE is triggered if the parent disagrees with an evaluation initiated by a public agency. The regulations also require that upon request for an IEE, the school must provide a parent with information on where an IEE may be obtained along with the applicable criteria (Smith Lee, 2004).

The school must set criteria that include the location of the evaluation and the qualifications of the examiner, which must be the same as the criteria the school uses when it initiates an evaluation. Other than these criteria, a school may not impose conditions or time lines related to a parent obtaining an IEE at public expense (Smith Lee, 2004).

In accordance with IDEA a school may publish a list of the names and addresses of evaluators that meet the criteria, including reasonable cost, as an effective way for agencies to inform parents of how and where they may obtain an IEE. To ensure a parent's right to an IEE, the parent, not the school, has the right to choose which evaluator will conduct the IEE. Districts must allow parents the opportunity to use an evaluator who is not on the list but who meets the criteria set forth by the school (Smith Lee, 2004).

When enforcing IEE criteria, schools must allow parents the opportunity to demonstrate that unique circumstances justify the selection of an evaluator that does not meet agency criteria. Students must be assessed in all areas related to the suspected disability, and there may be situations in which students need evaluations by evaluators who do not meet agency criteria. In these instances, the school must ensure that parents still have the right to the IEE at public expense and are informed about where the evaluations may be obtained (Smith Lee, 2004).

Amendment of Records

If a parent believes that the collected, maintained, or used information in a student's educational record is inaccurate, misleading, or violates the student's right to privacy, a request can be made by the parent to change the information (Legal Framework, 2015; US Department of Education, 2015b). While a school is not required to amend education records in accordance with a parent's request, the school is required to consider the request (US Department of Education, 2015a).

The school must decide whether to change the information within a reasonable time period; if the school refuses to change the information, it must inform the parent of the refusal and that a right to a hearing is available (Cornell Law School, n.d. k; US Department of Education, 2015b). If, as a result of the hearing, the school still does not amend the record, the parent has the right to insert a statement setting forth his or her views in the record. Statements must remain with the contested part of the student's record for as long as the record is maintained (US Department of Education, 2015b).

While the FERPA amendment procedure may be used to challenge facts that are inaccurately recorded, it may not be used to challenge a grade, an opinion, or a substantive decision made by the school about a student. Additionally, if FERPA's amendment procedures are not applicable to a parent's request for amendment, the school is not required to hold a hearing on the matter (US Department of Education, 2015b).

Hearing Procedures

State complaint. State complaint procedures are under direct control of the state education agency, and provide parents and school districts with procedures that allow for the resolution of differences without having to file a due process complaint. A state complaint may be filed by an organization or an individual, as opposed to mediation and due process, which require the child's parent or school system to initiate the process (Center for Parent Information and Resources, 2017). Violations alleged in the complaint must have occurred within one year before the date the complaint is received (Cornell Law School, n.d. d).

Complaints must be made in writing, signed, and include a statement demonstrating that the school district has violated a requirement of Part B of IDEA (IDEA Partnership, n.d.; Cornell Law School, n.d. d; Center for Parent Information and Resources, 2017). The statement must also include the facts on which the statement is based as well as the signature and contact information for the complainant (Cornell Law School, n.d. d; Center for Parent Information and Resources, 2017).

If the alleged violation is with respect to a specific child, the complaint must also include the name and address of the child, the name of his or her school, and a description, with facts, of the nature of the problem. A proposed resolution of the problem, to the extent known and available, by the complainant should also be included in the complaint at the time it is filed (Cornell Law School, n.d. d; Center for Parent Information and Resources, 2017).

State complaints must be resolved within sixty days from the date the complaint is filed unless an extension of the time line is permitted (Cornell Law School, n.d. d). As part of the resolution process an independent on-site investigation may be conducted (Center for Parent Information and Resources, 2017). In addition, the complainant has an opportunity to submit additional oral or written information about the complaint, and the SEA must provide the school with an opportunity to respond. Once all information has been gathered and reviewed, the SEA must make an independent determination on the complaint and issue a written decision to the complainant (Cornell Law School, n.d. d; Center for Parent Information and Resources, 2017).

Due process. Within fifteen calendar days after receiving a notice of due process complaint, and before the due process hearing begins, the school district must hold a resolution meeting with the parent and the relevant members of the IEP team who have specific knowledge of the facts identified in the due process complaint. The meeting must include a representative of the school district who has decision-making authority for the district and may not include an attorney representing the school district unless the parent is accompanied by an attorney (Cornell Law School, n.d. c).

The purpose of the meeting is for all parties to discuss the facts of the complaint and to provide the school district with the opportunity to resolve the dispute. The resolution meeting is not necessary if the parent and school district agree in writing to waive the meeting or if they agree to use the mediation process (Cornell Law School, n.d. c). Current student educational placement must be maintained when a due process complaint has been filed, during the resolution process, and while waiting for the decision of any impartial due process hearing unless the parent and school district agree otherwise (Cornell Law School, n.d. a).

If an agreement is not reached during a resolution meeting, the parent and school may continue discussions and work toward resolving the dispute and reaching an agreement. The parent may also ask for mediation, where a mediator would help facilitate communications with the school. If an agreement is still not reached within thirty calendar days of the filing of the due process complaint, the parent may proceed to the due process hearing (Center for Appropriate Dispute Resolution in Special Education, 2014).

A parent or school district may file a due process complaint on any matter relating to a proposal or refusal to initiate or change the identification, evaluation, or educational placement of a student or the provision of a free appropriate public education. Due process complaints must be filed within a two year period from the time that the alleged violation occurred or parents/ officials were made aware of such an action (Cornell Law School, n.d. c).

In order to request a hearing, a parent or school district must submit a due process complaint to the other party. Similar to a state complaint, the complaint must remain confidential and contain the name of the child, his or her address, and the name of the school. A description of the problem, including facts relating to the problem, and a proposed resolution must also be included (Cornell Law School, n.d. c).

Parents may have the right to represent themselves at a due process hearing. Depending on the state of residence, any party to a due process hearing has the right to be accompanied and advised by an attorney and/or nonattorney as well as to present evidence and confront, cross-examine, and require the attendance of witnesses or prohibit the introduction of any nondisclosed evidence at the hearing. Parents must also be given the right to have the student and/or public present at the hearing and have the record of the hearing, findings of fact, and decisions provided at no cost (Cornell Law School, n.d. e).

A trained, impartial hearing officer acting as a judge will listen to both sides and render a written decision on the case. The hearing officer's decision may be appealed by either party within ninety days of the decision. If the decision favors the parent and the school does not appeal, the decision becomes final and the school must follow the decision as soon as possible (Understood, 2017a).

Mediation. School districts are required to make mediation an option available to parents and the district to resolve disagreements involving any matter under Part B of IDEA (1990), including matters arising prior to the filing, whether or not a due process complaint to request a due process hearing has been filed (Cornell Law School, n.d. g).

Special education mediation is a voluntary and confidential process available at no cost when school personnel and parents disagree about the educational needs of a student with disabilities. During mediation, an impartial third-party facilitator helps parents and the school clarify any issues or underlying concerns, explore interests, discuss options, and reach mutually satisfying agreements addressing the needs of the student (Massachusetts Executive Office for Administration and Finance, 2017).

Disputes are resolved by the parents and school, not the mediator, in order to promote respect and a collaborative problem-solving effort between the family and the school community. The mediation process provides a structured approach that ensures all participants the ability to express their perspectives while being treated fairly and impartially, and often elicits a different outcome than what was reached in previous special education meetings (Massachusetts Executive Office for Administration and Finance, 2017).

CREATING AND LEADING AN EFFECTIVE STUDENT SUPPORT TEAM

The student support team (SST) is a school-based problem-solving team that provides support to teachers to improve the quality of the general education program and reduce the underachievement of students. SSTs have a vital role in enabling educators to teach students more effectively as well as in enabling students to acquire academic and social competencies, achieve standards, and become independent learners for life (Mugurussa, 2013).

Design of the Student Support Team

To successfully implement an effective SST, schools must cultivate and foster a collaborative culture in which all staff take responsibility for the success of all students (Massachusetts Department of Elementary and Secondary Education, n.d.). Core members of an SST are the overseers of the team process and promote general education teacher ownership. These members include the school principal, general educators, special education teachers and team chair, and family members of the student. The ancillary team members can provide specific expertise and may include the 504 coordinator, personnel from state agencies or community organizations, and/or the student (Department of Defense Educational Activity, 2007; Massachusetts Department of Elementary and Secondary Education, 2016).

Intervention teams succeed or fail based upon the group process employed to operate and function. An overarching goal of the SST should be shared leadership and full participation by all members of the team. A team coordinator can lead a successful and cohesive team by overseeing all planning and organizational activities, effectively communicating with other team members and serving as a contact to the school (Mugurussa, 2013).

It is important to note that case liaisons are responsible for meeting with the requesting educator to pinpoint the problem, gather data, and collaborate with other educators who may have additional clarifying information (Mugurussa, 2013).

Role of the Student Support Team

One of the primary goals of an SST is to increase the success of a student in the general education curriculum and within the general education classroom. The mission of the SST is to look at the whole child and consider data on the student's academic and nonacademic needs. Family members and school staff can bring forth any issue and seek input from an SST, which will suggest classroom-based, student/family-focused, or school-focused strategies and interventions. The intensity of these supports and/or interventions will vary depending on the individual student's needs (Massachusetts Department of Elementary and Secondary Education, 2016).

Another primary function of the team is routine, structured problem solving in conjunction with educators requesting assistance and the resolution of student-centered problems. Teams work effectively with other educators and staff members, analyze student problems, and design powerful interventions to effect the desired change (Mugurussa, 2013). SSTs are action oriented and maintain consistent communication and regularly scheduled meetings with a student's family in order to effectively engage in the problem-solving process (Massachusetts Department of Elementary and Secondary Education, 2016).

The SST does not determine eligibility for special education services nor is it a substitute for those services. What it does is make recommendations regarding the full continuum of interventions and services available at the school including accommodations under Section 504 of the Rehabilitation Act (Mugurussa, 2013).

CREATING AND MAINTAINING SCHOOL AND FAMILY PARTNERSHIPS

Effective parent engagement starts with giving attention to the strengths and needs of parents and aims to empower parents with the knowledge and skills needed to support a student's academic success (US Department of Education, 2016). Parents should be encouraged and helped to develop leadership skills that enable their participation in decision making.

Learned leadership skills will empower parents to design and conduct parent learning opportunities that cover how to access resources such as parent rights and responsibilities, school procedures, and any other information that will make parents feel informed and integrated into the school while supporting the well-being of the student (US Department of Education, 2016).

To encourage and maintain school-family partnerships, educators should examine a family's capacity to support a student's academic achievement and seek to increase awareness of instructional programs and methods that can be utilized to support student learning. A student's family should also understand how to participate in decisions to improve learning and advocate for student needs (US Department of Education, 2016).

Effective school-family relationships are strongly related to improved student learning, attendance, and behavior (Grant & Ray, 2016). Family involvement improves student success, regardless of race/ethnicity, class, or parents' level of education. Educators can foster an effective school-family relationship by recognizing and removing barriers to parent involvement as well as sharing decision making with parents and community members (National PTA, n.d.).

WORKING EFFECTIVELY WITH OUTSIDE AGENCIES

Community-school strategies recognize that public institutions share responsibility for helping children develop academically and become motivated and engaged in learning. It is imperative that schools and communities work together using a collaborative and comprehensive approach to have the most positive impact on the academic success of students.

Community partnerships can assist schools in preparing students for further education and future careers by offering additional opportunities and supports that are not traditionally found in a school system (Coalition for Community Schools, Institute for Educational Leadership & National Association of School Psychologists, 2016).

To foster a successful school-community partnership, it is beneficial to create a school leadership team consisting of the school principal, general and special education personnel, parents, students, and community leaders. It is critical that this leadership team guide the planning, implementation, and evaluation of the partnership to maximize effectiveness and sustainability (Coalition for Community Schools, Institute for Educational Leadership & National Association of School Psychologists, 2016).

The formation of a leadership team ensures a collaborative engagement in best practices between the school and community that will enhance preexisting school services. Community partners consist of community organizations concerned with the education of children, such as local government agencies, nonprofit organizations, and businesses and civic organizations, among others (Coalition for Community Schools, Institute for Educational Leadership & National Association of School Psychologists, 2016).

Delineation of roles and responsibilities and a clear set of expectations among school personnel and community partners can enhance the efficiency and effectiveness of service delivery while ensuring the needs of the school are being met. It is important to remember that the role of the community partner is to expand students' access to necessary opportunities, supports, and services and not to replace school educators or school-provided services (Coalition for Community Schools, Institute for Educational Leadership & National Association of School Psychologists, 2016).

Community partnerships enhance existing school-based resources and service delivery to help fill in the gaps based on the needs of the school. It is important for the leadership team to conduct assessments regarding the assets and needs of the school while forming a school-community partnership and throughout an existing partnership. An assessment examines the current resources that are available within the school where service delivery gaps exist (Coalition for Community Schools, Institute for Educational Leadership & National Association of School Psychologists, 2016).

Frameworks should then be established for outcomes that have specific short- and long-term goals based on the needs identified in the assessment. A comprehensive framework should intertwine existing school-based services and resources with resources needed from community partners (Coalition for Community Schools, Institute for Educational Leadership & National Association of School Psychologists, 2016). For example, if student depression and exposure to neighborhood violence after school are identified as two critical areas, the leadership team should develop short- and long-term goals to measure expected progress.

Assessing Partner Fit

Data from the needs assessment can be used to assess the fit of potential community partners. Strong candidates for partnership must be able to clearly articulate how they are able to enhance existing services and contribute to overall student success. Schools should not only choose partners that are necessary and fit with their needs, but continually assess their current partnerships (Coalition for Community Schools, Institute for Educational Leadership & National Association of School Psychologists, 2016).

Strategies for Building and Maintaining Successful Partnerships

Ensure a common vision among all partners. Both the school and community should be invested in a set of common visions and expectations to sustain long-term partnerships and enhance efficacy. Clearly defined roles must work collaboratively to ensure that the partnerships' vision and specific goals are in alignment with and integrated into the district's overall school improvement plan. To foster a successful sense of collaboration, community partners must adapt their mission to align with the community-school vision (Coalition for Community Schools, Institute for Educational Leadership & National Association of School Psychologists, 2016).

Establish formal relationships and collaborative structures. A fruitful and mutually beneficial school-community partnership relies on the active involvement of families, educators, educational boards, unions, local organizations, and state and local government agencies. Bringing partners on board and sustaining active involvement requires structured and collaborative opportunities such as developing task forces and reaching formal agreements (Coalition for Community Schools, Institute for Educational Leadership & National Association of School Psychologists, 2016).

Encourage open dialogue about challenges and solutions. Shared ownership is critical for sustaining a successful school-community relationship. Although schools are primarily responsible for ensuring every student is well-educated and prepared for a productive future, constructive engagement with community organizations is key to achieving better outcomes for students. Successful shared ownership requires collective trust among partners and the ability to discuss issues openly to find workable solutions (Coalition for Community Schools, Institute for Educational Leadership & National Association of School Psychologists, 2016).

Engage partners in the use of data. Targeted and useful data on school-community initiatives is necessary for measuring student, school, and family outcomes. Sharing data enables those involved to understand the status of measurable goals and provides accountability requiring visible progress on outcomes. External community partners can often bring new viewpoints on data that help schools evaluate existing partnerships and activities based on goals for achievement, attendance, and behavior (Coalition for Community Schools, Institute for Educational Leadership & National Association of School Psychologists, 2016).

Leveraging community resources and braiding funding streams. On average, only about one-quarter of all resources in community-school initiatives come from school districts. The remainder is garnered from other sectors such as local, state, and federal funding streams, foundations, and a variety of public agencies and community-based organizations (Coalition for Community Schools, Institute for Educational Leadership & National Association of School Psychologists, 2016).

Long-term sustainability. Successful partnerships plan for long-term sustainability by developing and creating diversified funding streams to support service delivery work. Continuous, high-quality professional development is instrumental to ensuring effective partnerships and should be aligned with the school improvement plan. Regular team-building exercises will create and solidify trustful relationships and ensure that all partners learn the same best practices (Coalition for Community Schools, Institute for Educational Leadership & National Association of School Psychologists, 2016).

FINAL THOUGHTS

Systemic change benefiting students with disabilities requires the involvement of parents, families, educators, community resources, other service providers, and organizations, to develop and implement comprehensive strategies that improve educational outcomes for children with disabilities (US Code, n.d. b).

The involvement of parents in the education of a student with disabilities is a legal right and is accompanied by certain protective procedural safeguards. Procedural safeguards such as prior written notice and consent are specific rules that ensure a parent knows what the school district is proposing to do and agrees with the plan. Options for resolution if a parent disagrees with the school include filing a state complaint, filing a due process complaint, attending a resolution meeting, and/or agreeing to mediation.

Family involvement is critical to the enduring success of a student not only in education but in attaining future goals. Acquiring leadership skills empowers parents to design, conduct, and seek out learning opportunities that address how to access resources, such as the rights and responsibilities discussed at the beginning of this chapter. Creating and maintaining effective school-family relationships removes barriers to parent involvement and are strongly correlated to improved student learning (Grant & Ray, 2015).

Student support teams are also in place to provide support to educators in improving the quality of the general education program and reducing the underachievement of students. Team members include not only the principal and special education teachers but also members of outside community organizations. Partnerships between the school and community prepare students for the future by providing additional opportunities and supports that are not traditionally found in school systems.

Collaboration between schools, parents and families, and outside agencies buttressed by student support teams can lead to astounding outcomes for students with disabilities. Students attend school consistently, are actively involved in learning, and are more successful in the long term. Families are increasingly involved in student learning and engaged with the school, thereby fostering a safe, supportive, and stable learning and living environment for the student.

POINTS TO REMEMBER

- *Schools must provide a parent with an opportunity to inspect and review a student's education records under FERPA (US Department of Education, 2015b). Educational records include transcripts, health records, tests, evaluations, discipline records, and records pertaining to special education eligibility or programs.*
- *Inaccurate or misleading information in the student's education records may be amended at the parent's request, although this right cannot be used to challenge grades, personal opinions, or substantive decisions made by a school about a student (US Department of Education, 2015b).*
- *Voluntary consent requires that an individual be fully informed of all information associated with a proposed action. Once given, consent can be withdrawn, in writing, at any point in time, including after a student has received special education services (Cornell Law School, n.d. b).*
- *State complaint procedures provide parents and school districts a mechanism for the resolution of differences, and the complaining party must demonstrate that a school district has violated a requirement of Part B of IDEA (IDEA Partnership, n.d.).*
- *Resolution meetings are held prior to a due process hearing for all parties to discuss the facts of the complaint and provide the opportunity to resolve the dispute. If the outcome of the resolution meeting is undesirable, a parent or school district may continue the due process complaint.*
- *Community partnerships prepare students for further education and future careers by offering additional opportunities and supports that are not traditionally found in a school system.*

Chapter Three

The Prereferral Process

Response to Intervention

Response to Intervention was originally developed to identify and prevent learning disabilities (Bjorn et al., 2016). RTI is a multilevel support system focused on early identification and support for struggling students in both the academic and behavioral arenas (Mitchell, Deshler, & Lenz, 2012). Students are identified as struggling through universal screenings and then provided with appropriate interventions (Hurlbut & Tunks, 2016; King Thorius et al., 2014; Kuo, 2015; Sansosti, Goss, & Noltemeyer, 2011).

Although the benefits of RTI are plentiful, there are challenges to its successful implementation. Lack of teacher training and support; varying viewpoints on who should provide interventions, monitor progress, and participate in RTI implementation, as well as understanding the differences between each tier, all contribute to disruptions in the flow of RTI. In addition to these challenges, education professionals continue to debate the effectiveness of a discrepancy model versus an RTI framework for identifying students with learning disabilities.

DEFINING RESPONSE TO INTERVENTION

The RTI framework first appeared as a means of identifying and preventing learning disabilities (Bjorn et al., 2016; King Thorius et al., 2014; Sansosti, Goss, & Noltemeyer, 2011). RTI has since evolved into a framework for ensuring that all students receive high-quality instruction through evidence-based interventions as soon as a weakness is discovered (Hoover & Sarris, 2014; King Thorius & Maxcy, 2015; Kuo, 2015).

RTI involves three tiers of support, which increase in intensity and frequency at the consecutive tiers. The first tier should meet the needs of approximately 80 percent of the student population. Tier I includes the use of evidence-based instructional practices, embedded principles of Universal Design for Learning, and differentiated instruction within the general education classroom (King Thorius et al., 2014; Kuo, 2015).

Tier II provides supports for students who have been identified as struggling in an academic and/or behavioral area. Tier II interventions include more intensive instruction focused on a targeted skill area and the use of evidence-based interventions, often occurring in small group settings (King Thorius et al., 2014). Tier II support is necessary for approximately 15 percent of the student population. Tier III interventions are applicable to approximately 5 percent of the student population. Interventions at this tier are more intensive in nature and can be conducted in small groups or one-on-one (Fuchs, Fuchs, & Compton, 2012).

RTI as a Federal Mandate

The Individuals with Disabilities Education Improvement Act and the Every Student Succeeds Act require the use of scientifically based practices, also known as evidence-based practices (US Department of Education, 2015a). The use of these instructional practices is at the heart of RTI (Hoover & Sarris, 2014; Hurlbut & Tunks, 2016; Hoppey, 2013; Kuo, 2015; Swanson et al., 2012). RTI has been acknowledged for its ability to ensure equity of educational resources and opportunities for all students, including those who have been previously underserved (Hoover & Sarris, 2014; King Thorius et al., 2014; Swanson et al., 2012).

Educator Responsibilities at Each Tier of the RTI Framework

Both general and special education teachers play a crucial role in the successful implementation of RTI. At tier I, the general education teacher is required by federal regulation to implement high-quality evidence-based instructional strategies. In addition, general education teachers are required to implement universal screenings, analyze data, and identify students who may require tier II supports (Bjorn et al., 2016).

Special education teachers may be involved in tier I in a consulting capacity. At tier II, special education teachers and other specialists, such as the reading specialist and/or speech therapist, may implement evidence-based interventions to small groups of identified students. Although similar to tier II, tier III consists of specialists engaged in evidence-based interventions at a more intense level (Leonard, 2012; Werts & Carpenter, 2013).

RTI can be implemented at every grade level as long as two critical components are met: clear performance expectations and methods for measuring student growth (or lack of growth) toward meeting the expectations (Sansosti, Goss, & Noltemeyer, 2011). Throughout all the tiers of RTI, educators collect and analyze student data. This data is used to make decisions about whether or not an intervention is working and whether more support—such as moving to a new tier or determining eligibility for special education services—is required (King Thorius & Maxcy, 2015; Swanson et al., 2012).

Special education teachers take on more responsibility as the implementation of RTI increases within school districts. These responsibilities include providing consultation to general education teachers, engaging in target interventions, and progress monitoring for students not on IEPs, as well as participating in RTI meetings (Bjorn et al., 2016; King Thorius & Maxcy, 2015).

Swanson and coauthors (2012) conducted a study of special education teachers and their viewpoints related to the benefits and challenges of RTI and their roles within the RTI framework. Starting with the benefits of RTI, special education teachers felt that the ability to identify the academic needs of students and to begin targeted interventions quickly was promising. In addition, special education teachers felt that being part of the early identification process was rewarding. A second benefit of RTI cited by special education teachers was the engagement in collaborative problem-solving and data analysis meetings with various colleagues, which special education teachers felt secured their role in the school community. Challenges of RTI acknowledged by special education teachers included increased paperwork, strained schedules due to larger caseloads, and the need for additional support staff.

Hoover and Sarris (2014) conducted a study examining highly qualified special education teachers' perceptions of the implementation of essential instructional roles within the RTI framework. The authors identified six instructional roles that are critical to the successful execution of the RTI framework: data-driven decision maker, implementer of evidence-based practices, implementer of social-emotional and behavioral supports, differentiator of instruction, implementer of instructional and assessment accommodations, and collaborator.

Data driven decision making and implementation of evidence-based practices are at the heart of the RTI framework. Addressing the emotional and behavioral needs of students in conjunction with their academic needs is another essential component to a comprehensive RTI framework. Differentiated instruction is the lifeblood of RTI, allowing for successful multitiered instruction at the core, supplemental, and intensive levels (Hoover & Sarris, 2014).

The role of instructional and assessment accommodator enables special education teachers to provide much-needed supports for students who struggle. Providing accommodations, in essence, levels the academic playing field for at-risk students. Collaboration is the final critical component of RTI. Collaboration with all stakeholders—including general education teachers, administration, paraprofessionals, and families—is vital to meeting the needs of a diverse student population (Hoover & Sarris, 2014).

Within these six essential roles, Hoover and Sarris found that differentiated instruction was the practice frequently engaged in by highly qualified special education teachers. On the flip side, implementation of evidence-based practices was the least frequent practice of special education teachers. This is alarming, as the use of evidence-based practices is specifically required under federal law, as well as supported as highly effective for diverse students by a vast majority of research (Hoover & Sarris, 2014).

A study conducted by Mitchell, Deshler, and Lenz (2012) examined the roles of special education teachers within a RTI framework. Their study revealed four key roles that special education teachers play within RTI: collaborator, interventionist, diagnostician, and manager. Closer examination of these roles revealed that special education teachers who engaged in RTI implementation devoted only 25 percent of their time to instruction. This presents a question as to whether special educators should be as heavily engaged in RTI or continue to focus mainly on those students identified as having a disability and requiring an IEP.

In addition to the 25 percent of instructional time mentioned above, special education teachers engaged in RTI implementation spend one-third of their time devoted to paperwork completion, one-quarter of their time engaged in collaborative efforts, and approximately 15 percent of their time analyzing assessment and progress-monitoring data to determine eligibility requirements (Mitchell, Deshler, & Lenz, 2012).

These statistics lend support to the ongoing conversation about whether special education teachers should be so involved in the RTI process. If general education teachers are required to be the primary providers of tier I and II supports, then it behooves teacher preparation programs and professional development opportunities to include more instruction on how to use evidence-based instructional strategies.

The Council for Exceptional Children (CEC), in its position statement on RTI, states that general education teachers should be the primary support, in consultation from special education teachers, through the first two tiers of RTI, while special education teachers should be providers of interventions within tier III only (CEC, 2014).

Challenges to Effectively Implementing RTI

Sansosti, Goss, and Noltemeyer (2011) conducted a study of special education administrators and their perspectives of RTI implementation within the secondary school setting. The results of the study identified several challenges. The first challenge, referred to as system structures, examines student schedules, lack of teacher time to engage in RTI activities, and lack of understanding of RTI procedures and implementation strategies.

The second challenge, roles and attitudes, refers to the mind-sets of professionals, parents, and community agencies. Specific recommendations suggest increased collaboration between educational professionals to increase the knowledge base of school principals and content-area secondary teachers around RTI, and increased information regarding RTI dispersed to community agencies as well as families (Sansosti, Goss, & Noltemeyer, 2011).

The final two challenges include a lack of implementation of evidence-based practices and inadequate teacher preparation and continued professional development. To address the lack of evidence-based practices, the implementation of universal screenings, scientifically based interventions, data collection techniques, and data-driven decision making should be increased within all educational settings. In conjunction with this, targeted professional development opportunities and teacher preparation programs need to explicitly focus on these measures (Sansosti, Goss, & Noltemeyer, 2011).

King Thorius and coauthors (2014) argue that there is a lack of sufficient RTI research supporting the consistent implementation of consistent high-quality instruction, that evidence-based interventions are supported by robust research, and that progress monitoring and interventions are sensitive to specific groups of learners.

TEACHER PREPARATION AND EXPOSURE TO RTI

RTI provides vital information to the prereferral process for special education eligibility. If preservice teachers, both general and special education, are prepared to include extensive exposure to evidence-based interventions, then the success of RTI implementation is promising (Hurlbut & Tunks, 2016).

Research suggests that general education teachers do not feel fully prepared to teach students with disabilities within inclusive classroom environments (Hurlbut & Tunks, 2016; McHatton & Parker, 2013). Further, research supports that preservice course work and field-based experiences in special education are critically important for promoting positive attitudes and feelings of competence when teaching students with disabilities (Atiles, Jones, & Kim, 2012; McHatton & Parker, 2013).

Hulbut and Tunks (2016) acknowledge the importance of explicit instruction as well as embedded components of RTI exposure within teacher preparation programs. Direct instruction in tier I interventions, instruction and practice in using assessment and progress-monitoring data, engagement in collaborative problem-solving techniques, and identification and implementation of evidence-based interventions and instructional strategies are necessary aspects of RTI that need to be taught extensively.

Neal (2013) conducted a study of preservice teachers and their perceptions of the training they received relative to RTI. The study found that special education preservice teachers attributed their ability to successfully implement services through RTI to the extensive hands-on field-based experiences they received from special education coursework. This finding supports the critical need for more special education courses for general education preservice teachers.

THE DISCREPANCY MODEL OR RESPONSE TO INTERVENTION

Prior to the widespread implementation of RTI, students were identified as having learning disabilities through a severe discrepancy model. The severe discrepancy model examined a student's intellectual ability across all domains and compared it to their academic functioning. If a severe discrepancy existed, the student was identified as having a learning disability. Some professionals and researchers felt that this model contributed to false identification and disproportionate labeling (Armendariz & Jung, 2016; King Thorius & Maxcy, 2015).

Armendariz and Jung (2016) conducted a study looking at the perspectives of educators (general and special) on acceptance of either the discrepancy model or the RTI model for identifying a learning disability. Results indicated that educators significantly preferred the RTI model over the discrepancy model. In addition, educators believed the RTI model was fair, provided reasonable assessment strategies, and assisted in developing meaningful learning goals.

As discussed previously, RTI encompasses an equity-focused framework that ensures high-quality instructional practices are provided to all students, adequate resources are available, and universal and student-focused progress monitoring happens. Despite the increasing use of RTI to identify learning disabilities, concerns linger regarding specificity around what constitutes adequate progress at each tier (Armendariz & Jung, 2016), which presents inconsistencies between states, districts, schools, and professionals.

FINAL THOUGHTS

RTI is a multilevel support system for struggling students. RTI incorporates universal screenings, evidence-based interventions, and progress monitoring through a collaborative school effort (Hurlbut & Tunks, 2016; King Thorius et al., 2014; Kuo, 2015; Sansosti, Goss, & Noltemeyer, 2011). Originally developed to identify students with learning disabilities, RTI has evolved to include prevention of learning deficits through remediation and early intervention.

The execution of RTI is not without its challenges. A lack of full understanding of the components and flow of RTI in addition to inconsistent implementation across states and districts presents ongoing problems. In addition, differing viewpoints on the effectiveness of a discrepancy model versus an RTI framework in identifying students with learning disabilities contributes to this inconsistency.

Increasing exposure to RTI components through explicit instruction, embedded assignments, and field-based experiences within teacher preparation programs and continued professional development opportunities once in the field may prove promising (Hurlbut & Tunks, 2016; McHatton & Parker, 2013).

POINTS TO REMEMBER

- *RTI is a multitiered support structure for students identified as struggling. The three tiers increase in intensity and intervention as well as who provides the services.*
- *RTI incorporates evidence-based interventions, progress monitoring, and collaboration to support struggling students.*
- *RTI ensures equitable distribution of educational resources to all students.*
- *RTI provides an alternative approach to identifying students with learning disabilities.*
- *Extensive exposure to RTI implementation during teacher preparation and professional development is vital to its success.*

Chapter Four

Writing Effective Individualized Education Plans

Every student who has a documented disability and requires specialized instruction and services to make effective progress in the general curriculum is required under the Individuals with Disabilities Education Improvement Act to have an Individualized Education Plan (US Department of Education, 2007). The IEP is the most critical document for students with disabilities identified as requiring special education services.

The IEP is individualized to meet the unique learning needs of the student. IEPs are written by a team that brings together the knowledge of all stakeholders working with the student, including teachers, parents or guardians, educational specialists, the student (over age fourteen), and others. Team members work together to develop an educational plan that will ensure positive educational outcomes for the student.

The IEP guides the delivery of services and supports the student requires to progress within the general curriculum. Federal law mandates particular components that must be incorporated within the IEP document; states then have the ability to add additional information as they see fit.

INDIVIDUALIZED EDUCATION PLAN COMPONENTS

The federally required components of an IEP include current performance levels, annual goals, special education and related services, participation with nondisabled peers, participation in state- and district-wide tests, dates and places where services will occur, transition service needs, needed transition services, age of majority, and how progress will be measured (US Department of Education, 2007). Each component ensures that students with learning disabilities will receive the best education possible.

Current Performance

Current performance, also referred to as *present levels of educational performance*, reveals how the student is doing in school. This section includes assessment data from curriculum-based measures, eligibility assessments, observational data, school attendance, and state- and district-wide testing, as well as identifying interests and personal characteristics. The other piece to this section is a statement describing how the student's disability interferes with the learning process and prevents the student from making effective progress (US Department of Education, 2007).

Annual Goals

Annual goals are targets that the student is expected to meet at the end of a particular year. The annual goals can include academic, behavioral, social, and daily living skills development, or any other educational need. Annual goals are broken down into smaller steps or objectives to assist the student in making slow, steady progress (US Department of Education, 2007). It is important that goals and objectives are measurable, as progress is measured through data collection. Progress toward goal achievement is monitored closely and frequently.

Special Education and Related Services

Special education and related services list the supports the student requires to be academically, socially, and behaviorally successful. Supports may include accommodations, modifications, changes to the curriculum, evidence-based instructional strategies, supplemental aids, and assessment modifications (US Department of Education, 2007).

Participation with Nondisabled Peers

IDEIA mandates that students with disabilities receive education and special education services in the least restrictive environment (LRE), which in many cases is in the general education classroom. However, there are times and instances in which a student with a disability may be better served by removal from the general education classroom into a smaller, more intensive setting, even for a short period of time. If this occurs, there must be a statement in the student's IEP that explains why removal from the general education classroom is justified (US Department of Education, 2007).

Participation in State- and District-Wide Assessments

Students with disabilities are held to the same academic standards as their nondisabled peers. As a result, modifications and accommodations must be provided to students to level the playing field on state- and district-wide assessments. This section of the IEP specifically states the types of accommodations the student will receive when participating in state or district assessments. If an assessment is not appropriate for a student, the special education team must write a statement explaining why the student is not able to participate in the assessment (US Department of Education, 2007).

Service Delivery Grid

The service delivery grid lists the specific services provided, as well as the frequency and location (such as a push-in service that is provided in the regular education classroom or a pull-out service that occurs in a separate room). The grid also delineates who will provide the services; for example, a speech goal may require a speech and language pathologist, while a reading or math goal may require a special education teacher. This section also identifies the start and end dates for the services to be provided (US Department of Education, 2007).

Transition Service Needs

Once a student turns fourteen he or she becomes a required member of the IEP team. Students at this age have a voice in their educational journey. A transition statement or plan is written describing the student's postsecondary goals. In addition, the IEP team must identify the courses and services the student will need in order to meet these goals. Once a student turns sixteen, specific transition services are identified and embedded into the IEP. Transition services assist students with preparing to leave the secondary education setting and enter into the workplace or a postsecondary environment (US Department of Education, 2007).

Age of Majority

The year before a student reaches the age of majority, which varies by state, the local educational agency must inform the student of his or her educational rights and the transfer of those rights once he or she reaches the age of majority (US Department of Education, 2007).

Measuring Progress

The IEP must clearly state how a student's progress toward meeting his or her annual goals will be measured. The IEP also communicates the frequency and amount of time to be devoted to the interventions and supports offered, and how parents and guardians will be informed of their child's progress (US Department of Education, 2007). Most school districts send progress reports home on the same cycle as report cards.

WRITING MEASURABLE IEP GOALS

In order to write an effective IEP goal, the team must ask three questions:

1. What is the student's starting point?
2. Where is the student going?
3. How is the student going to get there? (Graves & Graves, 2016)

Knowing the student's current performance level will help answer the first question. The team needs to know what the student can currently do in relation to a specific content area, skill, behavioral, or social domain. This current performance provides a benchmark from which goals will be built.

Depending on the goal, the team will also need to know where the student should be in relation to grade-level standards, normally developing peers, and so on. The goal must be realistic and attainable within the specified period. It is also important to identify the steps (objectives), supports, services, frequency, and providers needed to assist the student with goal obtainment (Graves & Graves, 2016).

Once the three questions have been discussed and answered, it is time to write the goal. When writing IEP goals, teams should also consider several things that should be incorporated. It is important to use terminology that all individuals can understand; parents and noneducation professionals may be reading a child's IEP. The IEP should be explicit about precisely what will be measured and how, it should identify how frequently to review performance, and who is responsible for examining the student's progress (Graves & Graves, 2016).

IEP goals should be written as SMART goals: goals that are specific, measurable, attainable, results-focused, and time limited (Heitin, n.d.; Wright, 2010). When IEP goals incorporate these components and are developed following the SMART acronym, it is easy for professionals and families to envision the beginning, middle, and end for their student and child.

Below are some examples of IEP goals. The goals are first written as broad and unclear, then as SMART goals that provide concise information.

Example 1: The student will write at grade level, with no errors in spelling or punctuation.
Example 1 written as a SMART goal: The student will write a paragraph with at least five sentences, each greater than seven words, with no more than one spelling error and with proper punctuation.

Example 2: With the aid of a multiplication chart, the student will be able to solve multiplication problems.
Example 2 written as a SMART goal: With the aid of a multiplication chart, the students will solve two-digit by one-digit multiplication problems with 90 percent accuracy.

Example 3: During small-group instruction, the student will display good eye contact with others.
Example 3 written as a SMART goal: During small-group instruction, the student will look at the teacher 80 percent of the time, in four out of five opportunities.

Example 4: The student will improve his or her reading.
Example 4 written as a SMART goal: The student will read a grade-level passage orally at a fluency rate of 115–130 words per minute with fewer than five errors.

THE CRITICAL NEED TO ESTABLISH EXIT CRITERIA FROM SPECIAL EDUCATION

The goal of both special and regular education is to provide support for each student to become "a skillful, free, and purposeful person, able to plan and manage his or her own life, and to reach his or her highest potential as an individual and as a member of society" (CEC, 2014). Special education can enhance the regular education learning environment to meet the needs of all learners (CEC, 1997). With the increased diversity in today's classrooms, one could make the argument that each student, disability or not, has a unique way of learning and requires that educators teach to his or her preferred learning style.

According to the National Center for Educational Statistics, only 65 percent of students with disabilities graduate from high school, compared to 83 percent of all students and 76 percent of economically disadvantaged students (US Department of Education, Office of Elementary and Secondary Education, 2015). Approximately 11 to 17 percent of students with disabilities do not receive a regular high school diploma but rather a certificate of completion or a modified diploma, signaling that they did not meet the standards for graduation (NCES, 2017a). Further, only approximately 35 percent of adults with disabilities are engaged in steady employment (NCES, 2017b).

These alarming statistics suggest that not only special education but also general education needs to change. Ultimately these figures suggest that schools are doing a disservice to students with disabilities. Special education has processes in place to ensure that students are making adequate progress toward their IEP goals, which must be aligned to state standards. Aligning IEP goals ensures that students are making progress toward grade-level standards with the appropriate supports. Another measure embedded in special education is a reevaluation to meet eligibility criteria every three years or sooner if needed. It was never intended for students, except those who are severely disabled, to stay on IEPs; rather the intention of special education is for students to learn and develop the skills they need to be successful and independent.

FINAL THOUGHTS

The IEP is the most critical document for students identified with disabilities who require services in order to make academic progress. Every student who qualifies for special education services must have a signed and accepted IEP in place before services can begin.

Federal law sets forth required components within the IEP, including the student's current educational performance levels, realistic annual goals and objectives, special education and related services, and a statement of participation with nondisabled peers. Other federally mandated components include involvement in state- and district-wide tests, the dates and locations where services will take place, transition needs and services, a statement of age of majority, and how student progress will be measured (US Department of Education, 2007).

SMART IEP goals are specific, measurable, attainable, results-focused, and time limited (Graves & Graves, 2016). Goals and objectives that include SMART components provide clarity to all stakeholders. Having clearly written goals and objectives supports progress-monitoring techniques, provides critical data for the IEP team, and assists the student in meeting his or her end result.

Alarming graduation and employment statistics for students with disabilities indicate the dire need for a change in the way individuals see special education. Approximately 35 percent of students with disabilities do not graduate from high school. Of that 35 percent, approximately 17 percent do not receive a high school diploma but rather a certificate of completion or modified diploma (NCES, 2017a). Employment statistics for individuals with disabilities are just as bleak.

POINTS TO REMEMBER

- *All students identified as having a disability and who qualify for special education services require a written Individualized Education Plan (IEP).*
- *Federal requirements ensure certain components within the IEP. These include current performance levels, annual goals and objectives, special education and related services, statement of participation with nondisabled peers, involvement in state- and district-wide tests, the dates and locations where services will take place, transition needs and services, age of majority statement, and how progress will be measured.*
- *IEP goals and objectives must be written as SMART goals to ensure measurability.*
- *There is a desperate need to clearly establish exit criteria from special education.*

Chapter Five

Creating Safe Learning Communities

*Addressing the Social and Emotional Needs of
Students with Learning Disabilities*

Nearly 2.4 million students are identified as having learning disabilities, which may result in academic, behavioral, social, or emotional difficulties (McGovern, Lowe, & Hill, 2016; National Center for Learning Disabilities, 2014). Research suggests that students who are identified as having learning disabilities are at an increased risk for experiencing heightened symptoms of both anxiety and depression; thus, it is imperative for educators to gain the knowledge and skills to create positive learning environments that develop the whole child (Mammarella et al., 2016).

The identified link between learning disabilities and emotional disturbances such as anxiety requires that teachers become familiar with, and incorporate strategies for, supporting these students by creating classroom environments where students feel safe. Research has proven that students with learning disabilities struggle to gain social competence, experience difficulties maintaining adequate peer relationships, have lower self-esteem, and display anxious and depressive symptoms (McGovern, Lowe, & Hill, 2016; Tannock, 2013).

Engaging in practices such as social and emotional learning, mindfulness and meditation, responsive classrooms, anti-bullying curricula, and positive behavioral supports have proven successful in creating safe learning environments for all students, including those with learning disabilities (Gueldner & Feuerborn, 2016; Meiklejohn et al., 2012; Milligan, Badali, & Spiroiu, 2015). These practices provide students with tools, strategies, and environments that support positive learning outcomes and social competence, and encourage healthy peer relationships.

LEARNING DISABILITIES AND MENTAL HEALTH CONCERNS

Specific learning disabilities are the largest classification of students receiving services under special education, at approximately 42 percent (National Center for Learning Disabilities, 2014; US Department of Education, 2014). Research indicates that adolescents identified as having learning disabilities present with a variety of difficulties, including academic, behavioral, social, and emotional (McGovern, Lowe, & Hill, 2016).

There is also an association between learning disabilities and emotional dysregulation. Students with learning disabilities encounter challenges processing information, which puts them at a higher risk for experiencing mental health problems (Mammarella et al., 2016; Milligan, Badali, & Spiroiu, 2015; Nelson & Harwood, 2011).

Within the behavioral and emotional domains, students with learning disabilities are twice as likely as students without learning disabilities to experience both internalizing and externalizing symptoms. Children and adolescents with learning disabilities tend to have lower social standing and less social support than peers without learning disabilities (McGovern, Lowe, & Hill, 2016). The use of coping tools and strategies to lessen the occurrence of challenging emotions and experiences have been supported through the literature (Milligan, Badali, & Spiroiu, 2015).

Classroom Concerns

Most teachers understand that learning disabilities can negatively affect academic achievement; however, students with learning disabilities often experience difficulties that extend beyond academics, including emotional and social spheres such as low academic self-confidence, feelings of rejection and neglect, anxiety, and unstable peer relationships (Milligan, Badali, & Spiroiu, 2015; Espelage, Rose, & Polanin, 2016; Tannock, 2013). It is estimated that approximately 30 to 50 percent of students with learning disabilities develop anxiety and depression symptoms, compared with only 10 to 20 percent of adolescents without learning disabilities (Ashraf & Najam, 2015; Malow, 2015).

Students with learning disabilities suffer bouts of anxiety throughout their educational experience and well into adulthood (Beauchemin, Hutchins, & Patterson, 2008; Nelson & Harwood, 2011). Many of these students are aware of the struggles they experience as a result of their learning disabilities (Malow, 2015). Some researchers suggest that learning difficulties produce anxiety symptoms. Academic success is a major developmental task to be accomplished throughout the school years, and students who struggle to master content due to a learning disability frequently encounter anxiety as a result of their academic struggles and possible failure (Nelson & Harwood, 2011).

Other researchers suggest that learning disabilities are the result of severe episodes of anxiety (Nelson & Harwood, 2011). Higher levels of anxiety experienced by students with learning disabilities greatly inhibit academic growth by work avoidance and/or attentional issues during the learning process (McGovern, Lowe, & Hill, 2016). Research has shown that these high levels of anxiety can produce negative effects on cognitive performance.

Dealing with anxiety requires cognitive energy, which limits the storage component of the processing system. This can be extremely exhausting for students with learning disabilities (Malow, 2015; McGovern, Lowe, & Hill, 2016; Nelson & Harwood, 2011). It is critical for educators to acknowledge that deficits in specific cognitive abilities such as working memory and metacognition are common characteristics of learning disabilities, and offer consistent support to reduce this pressure (McGovern, Lowe, & Hill, 2016; Swanson & Sachse-Lee, 2001).

Approximately 70 percent of students with learning disabilities develop symptoms of anxiety at a much higher rate than their peers (Nelson & Harwood, 2011). Because of this, teachers should be aware that students with learning disabilities are at risk for displaying anxiety-related distress within the school setting. Teachers should be trained and supported in creating safe learning environments in order to accommodate these students (McGovern, Lowe, & Hill, 2016; Milligan, Badali, & Spiroiu, 2015; Nelson & Harwood, 2011).

Educational professionals acknowledge that the emotional needs of students with learning disabilities often go neglected. Services tend to be focused on the academic needs of the learning disability (Nelson & Harwood, 2011). Understanding the symptomology of anxiety that is experienced by students with learning disabilities will assist teachers in identifying and providing appropriate interventions that reduce anxiety while supporting academic gains (Tannock, 2013; Zenner, Herrnleben-Kurz, & Walach, 2014).

In addition to the connection between learning disabilities and anxiety, research has linked learning disabilities with an increased appearance of depression. Students who tend to perform poorly at school and fail to achieve expected academic outcomes have a higher risk of current and long-term psychological maladjustment, including internalizing disorders such as depression, anxiety, and social withdrawal. Students with nonverbal learning disabilities report increased anxiety levels, as well as separation anxiety and depressive symptoms pertaining to school (Mammarella et al., 2016). Students with reading disabilities such as dyslexia experience higher depressive symptoms than their nondisabled peers (Dahle, Knivsberg, & Andressen, 2011).

It is critical that teachers include anxiety-reducing measures into their classroom environments. Having strategies in place to reduce the symptoms of anxiety proves to be beneficial to all students, including those with disabilities (Malow, 2015). Teachers can accomplish this in simple ways. Scheduling five- to ten-minute anxiety-reducing breaks that focus on deep breathing, yoga poses, or visualization is one example of an effective strategy.

Teachers need to be aware that anxiety tends to worsen during unstructured times as well as during academic tasks in areas where students' disabilities impede learning. Being proactive with alternative options such as small-group activities, providing additional time for students to process information and respond, and providing tools that support self-regulation all assist students in managing their anxieties and being successful students (Malow, 2015).

Gender Considerations

Studies indicate that the occurrence of anxiety and depressive symptoms are more prevalent among students with learning disabilities at a percentage of almost 40 percent (Ashraf & Najam, 2015; National Center for Learning Disabilities, 2014). Adolescent students with learning disabilities combined with emotional dysregulation may present with significantly high symptoms of phobic disorders, generalized anxiety, and significant depressive symptoms (Ashraf & Najam, 2015; Alesi, Rappo, & Pepo, 2014). In addition, students with learning disabilities comorbid with anxiety and depression, who do not receive therapy to reduce their symptoms, will experience negative outcomes through life. If left untreated, anxiety and depression can impact their life as evidenced by severe internalizing behaviors including suicidal attempts (Ashraf & Najam, 2015; Alesi, Rappo, & Pepo, 2014).

BEYOND ACADEMICS: SUPPORTING THE WHOLE STUDENT

Preparing students to be twenty-first-century learners is significant to educational reform. Twenty-first-century skills are embedded through the development of cognitive, interpersonal, and personal confidence (National Research Council, 2012). Social and emotional learning is a significant movement in the realm of education reform and can serve as a way of increasing prosocial skills development and positive academic outcomes (Espelage, Rose, & Polanin, 2016).

Practicing mindfulness, yoga, and meditation has proven to mitigate many of the symptoms of stress and to increase self-esteem and positivity. Studies suggest that these practices lead to improved student outcomes. Teaching students to practice self-care impacts their social-emotional development, allowing them to successfully navigate the often confusing emotional landscape.

Social-Emotional Learning

Social-emotional learning has been linked to increased academic performance and increased resiliency for all students, especially those with disabilities (Durlak et al., 2011). Understanding the impact emotional health has on academic performance will better prepare schools and teachers to identify supports to address the whole child and not simply academic performance (Gueldner & Feuerborn, 2016).

Social-emotional instruction promotes five person-centered interrelated components: self-awareness, self-management, social awareness, relationship skills, and responsible decision making. These skills are essential to the development of cognitive, social, and emotional development of students (Collaborative for Academic, Social and Emotional Learning, 2017).

Part of social-emotional learning includes instruction in bullying prevention. It is estimated that 25 percent of elementary, 34 percent of middle school, and 26 percent of high school students with disabilities are victims of bullying (Blake et al., 2012). The employment of a social-emotional curriculum for addressing instances of bullying by proactively teaching prosocial attitudes such as empathy has been established as beneficial to all students (Espelage, Rose, & Polanin, 2016).

There are many social-emotional curricula in public schools throughout the country. One well-known curriculum is Second Step, which has three programs, one for each grade range: early learning, elementary, and middle school. Each teaches students about prosocial attitudes and behaviors, school belonging, and academic achievement (Espelage, Rose, & Polanin, 2016).

Espelage and coauthors (2016) conducted a study using the SS-SSTP with middle school students with learning disabilities. The results of the study indicated clinically significant findings. Students with learning disabilities who were exposed to social-emotional learning through SS-SSTP displayed higher rates of prosocial behavior, including intervening in instances of bullying, as well as increased academic performance.

In addition to the SS-SSTP curriculum, a cyberbullying prevention curriculum called Steps to Respect is available through the same company. This program, which consists of five lessons and includes a family component, focuses solely on the dangers of cyberbullying and how to implement prevention strategies (Committee for Children, 2013). With the rise in the occurrence of cyberbullying, this program would prove beneficial in any elementary, middle, or high school. The lessons and resources are free for download on the company's website.

A wide range of social-emotional programs, curricula, and strategies are available to support schools in developing safe learning environments. Several social-emotional programs worth exploring are mentioned here:

- The Morningside Center for Teaching Social Responsibility is an organization that supports schools in creating safe, collaborative, and respectful learning communities. They provide various resources, including lessons, videos, training, and articles (moringsidecenter.org).
- The Inner Resilience Program offers K–8 programs for teaching mindfulness practices within the classroom. These programs provide teachers with the resources they need for effective implementation. The organization also offers support for families in the form of workshops (innerresilience.org).
- Open Circle is an evidence-based K–5 social-emotional program focused on helping students develop skills in relation to emotion identification, building positive peer relationships, developing empathy, and encouraging problem-solving skills. Teachers are supported through lesson plans and resources (open-circle.org).

Mindfulness, Meditation, and Yoga

There continues to be an increased interest in the implementation of mindfulness practices to promote wellness within the schools. Mindfulness strategies include meditation, breathing techniques, and yoga. These routines have been shown to remediate problem behavior and promote well-being for students with mental health problems such as anxiety and depression (Meiklejohn et al., 2012).

A meta-analysis of twenty-four school-based mindfulness programs focused on teaching relaxation and coping skills to all students indicates that mindfulness interventions have positive outcomes on students' ability to focus, regulate self-control, and ultimately make academic gains (Zenner, Herrnleben-Kurz, & Walach, 2014).

A qualitative study of the effects of Integra Mindfulness Martial Arts (MMA) to support self-regulation challenges for students with learning disabilities was conducted by Milligan, Badali, and Spiroiu (2015). Integra MMA is an evidence-informed intervention that combines mindfulness, cognitive therapy, and behavior modification into a martial arts training program. The results indicate that adolescents felt that learning and participating in the mindfulness practices provided strategies that they could use to decrease patterns of emotional dysfunction and self-regulate their behavior.

A 2008 study conducted by Beauchemin, Hutchins, and Patterson looked at the impact of mindfulness and meditation intervention on anxiety levels of high school students diagnosed with learning disabilities. The study consisted of ten minutes of meditation at the beginning of each class period, five days per week, for five consecutive weeks. Once completed, the study revealed significant decreases in anxiety symptoms and, therefore, cognitive interference, which yielded positive academic outcomes in all participants (Beauchemin, Hutchins, & Patterson, 2008; Gueldner & Feuerborn, 2016).

Programs that teach mindfulness-based strategies can fall under the umbrella of social-emotional learning. Although mindfulness-based practices are unique in that they incorporate yoga, meditation, and breathing techniques, these practices offer similarities to components in social-emotional learning. Both mindfulness-based practices and social-emotional instruction occur within the school/classroom setting during a specific designated time, provide options for out-of-school/out-of-classroom practice, include the use of supportive materials such as videos and handouts, and can include parents and families in promoting practices at home (Gueldner & Feuerborn, 2016).

FINAL THOUGHTS

Students who present with combined deficits in academic performance and mental health symptoms are entering classrooms at an alarming rate (National Center for Learning Disabilities, 2014). This, in conjunction with the knowledge that learning disabilities have a higher comorbid rate of anxiety and depressive symptoms, requires increased awareness and support within the schools (Nelson & Harwood, 2011).

Mindfulness-based strategies such as yoga and meditation as well as social-emotional programs offer beneficial practices for decreasing the symptoms of anxiety and depression in students with learning disabilities (Gueldner & Feuerborn, 2016; Milligan, Badali, & Spiroiu, 2015; Zenner, Herrnleben-Kurz, & Walach, 2014). Mindfulness, meditation, and yoga techniques in the classroom provide simple ways to support all students by providing tools and strategies that can be used to regulate behavior (Meiklejohn et al., 2012).

Social-emotional curricula incorporate exposure to areas that address the cognitive, social, and emotional development of all students (Collaborative for Academic, Social and Emotional Learning, 2017). In order to address the development of these skills, social-emotional instruction integrates instruction in self-awareness, self-management, social awareness, relationship skills, and responsible decision-making skills. Instruction in these areas has proven effective in supporting increased academic achievement (National Research Council, 2012).

POINTS TO REMEMBER

- *Forty-two percent of school-aged children are identified as having learning disabilities (National Center for Learning Disabilities, 2014).*
- *Thirty to fifty percent of students identified as having a learning disability experience mental health issues (Ashraf & Najam, 2015; Malow, 2015).*
- *Symptoms of anxiety and/or depression that are not addressed early tend to become more severe over time and negatively impact adulthood.*
- *Social-emotional instruction, meditation, and mindfulness practices are examples of effective ways to reduce the symptoms of anxiety and depression and to regulate behavior for all students, especially those with learning disabilities.*

Chapter Six

Evidence-Based Instructional Strategies

Meeting the Needs of Students with Learning Disabilities

High academic standards, the pressure to raise student outcomes, and a wide range of ability levels within inclusive classrooms, necessitate the implementation of evidence-based instructional practices (Maheady et al., 2016). Federal mandates, including the Individuals with Disabilities Education Improvement Act of 2004 and the Every Student Succeeds Act, require that all teachers identify and incorporate evidence-based instructional practices within their classrooms in order to support increased academic achievement (US Department of Education, 2015a).

Another significant principle under IDEIA is that children with exceptionalities are entitled to receive special education services in the least restrictive environment, which in many cases is the general education classroom. Children with exceptionalities bring a diverse set of needs, challenges, and dynamics into the general education classroom. The mandate that they be educated in the least restrictive environment creates an indispensable need for educators to be fluent in evidence-based instructional strategies and models. These strategies and models are available to support students with learning disabilities within inclusion classrooms across all content areas.

The continuous use of evidence-based instructional practices is key to providing appropriate, high-quality instruction for students with disabilities (Maheady et al., 2016). Extensive research confirms that evidence-based instructional practices, when used with fidelity, can close the achievement gap by optimizing student outcomes (Scheeler, Budin, & Markelz, 2016; Institute of Education Sciences, n.d.).

Evidence-based practices are instructional strategies that have been proven effective through extensive and methodologically sound research studies (CEC, 2014). Disturbing statistics indicate that not all practitioners have been trained on how to identify practices considered to be evidence based (Chiang et al., 2017). This alarming indicator presents a critical area for improvement in teacher preparation programs as well as professional development opportunities. The literature suggests that there are several strategies teacher preparation programs and school districts can develop to address this disconnect (Scheeler, Budin, & Markelz, 2016).

DETERMINATION OF EVIDENCE-BASED SPECIAL EDUCATION PRACTICES

To be considered an evidence-based practice, an intervention or strategy must be supported by strong evidence and credible research. The research must demonstrate that the intervention or practice results in positive student outcomes and must be be specific to a learning area, such as reading fluency, and specific to a population of students, for example, students with dyslexia (CEC, 2014; Institute of Education Sciences, n.d.). For an intervention to have strong evidence to support its effectiveness, studies must be well designed and employ either randomized controlled trials, comparison group studies, or single-subject research studies (CEC, 2014).

Quality of evidence refers to how meritoriously a study was carried out. The experiment should identify every aspect of the study, including who implemented the study, who participated in the study, how the intervention differed from the control group, and a discussion of how the outcomes will affect future research. Further, the results of a study must have reliability and validity to ensure accurate outcomes (Chiang et al., 2017).

In 2014 the Council for Exceptional Children prepared a set of standards that included quality indicators and classifications for evidence-based practices. The distinct classifications are: evidence-based practices, potentially evidence-based practices, practices having mixed effects, practices having negative effects, and practices having insufficient evidence to categorize their effectiveness (Browder et al., 2014; CEC, 2014).

The quality indicators developed by the CEC, which must be present for an instructional practice to be considered evidence based, include context and setting, participants, intervention agent, description of practice, implementation fidelity, internal validity, outcome measures and dependent variables, and data analysis (Browder et al., 2014; CEC, 2014; Harn, Parisi, & Stoolmiller, 2013).

In addition to the CEC standards, the Institute of Educational Sciences (Chiang et al., 2017) established rating criteria to determine the effectiveness of instructional strategies and interventions. The identification criteria place a strategy or intervention into one of the following categories: positive effects, potentially positive effects, mixed effects, potentially negative effects, negative effects, and no discernible effects (Kratochwill et al., 2013; Institute of Education Sciences, n.d.).

EVIDENCE-BASED INSTRUCTIONAL STRATEGIES

A plethora of instructional strategies exist to help struggling students and those with learning disabilities; most are evidence-based strategies, although some non-evidence-based strategies have also been found to directly benefit students. Evidence-based strategies can be monitored for effectiveness though the Response to Intervention process. A sampling of evidence-based strategies follows.

Differentiated Instruction

Differentiated instruction refers to a teaching approach that takes into account the content, the learning process, learning styles, presentation strategies, and assessment techniques in order to provide students with the individualized structure to maximize strengths, accommodate weaknesses, and provide for immediate feedback (British Columbia Ministry of Education & British Columbia School Superintendent's Association, 2011).

Scruggs, Mastropieri, and Marshak (2012) define *differentiated instruction* as supplying students with the instructional strategies and materials that meet their individual learning needs. In addition, teachers must remain flexible in their instructional approaches and curricula in order to support differentiation (Obiakor et al., 2012).

Key aspects of differentiation include maintaining flexibility in student engagement opportunities as well as instructional approaches, proactive planning for learning styles and interests, and providing multiple pathways for learning (Tomlinson, 2014). Differentiation is similar to a UDL framework in that teachers provide multiple avenues by which students can take in information, engage with the learning process, and show what they understand.

The goals of differentiated instruction include the explicit explanation of concepts, the use of assessment as an instructional guide, supporting students in developing critical-thinking skills, and providing opportunities for students to actively engage in the learning process (Tomlinson, 2014).

Co-Teaching

Co-teaching is an instructional model that brings together a special education teacher and a general education teacher, who share their expertise, collaborate, and address the learning needs of their students together (Solis et al., 2012). There are five evidence-based models for implementing co-teaching: one teach, one assist; station teaching; parallel teaching; alternative teaching; and team teaching (Teachers College, n.d.).

Across the various co-teaching models, one critical aspect is that two highly qualified teachers are present in the classroom. Each teacher provides one aspect of instruction support for the benefit of all students. In addition, the co-teaching model supports the practice of inclusiveness within the schools (Teachers College, n.d.).

Direct and Explicit Instruction

Direct instruction, also known as explicit instruction, is an instructional technique where a strategy, skill, or specific content is taught precisely by the teacher (Archer & Hughes, 2011). Here, the teacher gives specific explanations or directions while also providing students with guidance and reinforcement through the learning process (Archer & Hughes, 2011; British Columbia Ministry of Education & British Columbia School Superintendent's Association, 2011).

There are several steps that ensure direct instruction is effective for students. First, the teacher makes sure that the learning objective is clearly stated and that students know what is expected and why. Once the objective is stated and explained, the teacher explicitly explains the concept, skill, or strategy that is being introduced. Next, the teacher models the skill or strategy.

After the first three steps occur, students are ready to actively engage in learning. Students are guided and supported through the use of frequent check-ins, self-evaluation and reflection, and time for independent practice (Archer & Hughes, 2011; British Columbia Ministry of Education & British Columbia School Superintendent's Association, 2011).

Universal Design for Learning

Universal Design for Learning (UDL) is an evidence-based framework that combines research in the fields of neuroscience and education (Meyer, Rose, & Gordon, 2014). UDL is a proactive way of planning by integrating supports and choices into the curriculum and classroom; it consists of three principles: multiple means of representation, multiple means of expression, and multiple means of engagement. In the next chapter we will discuss UDL in greater detail (National Center on Universal Design for Learning, 2017).

Peer-Mediated Instruction

In many classrooms, students serve as role models and/or peer instructors to other students in the educational environment; this is commonly referred to as peer-mediated instruction. Peer-mediated instruction is an instructional model that has been proven effective in inclusion classrooms and is well documented in the literature (Ford, 2013). Peers can provide two forms of instruction: direct and indirect.

Direct peer instruction is similar to tutoring, while indirect peer instruction occurs through modeling. When using peer-mediated instruction, teachers take on the role of facilitator rather than providing the primary source of instruction. One example of a well-known and frequently used elementary peer-mediated strategy is known as Peer-Assisted Learning Strategies (PALS).

EVIDENCE-BASED READING STRATEGIES FOR STUDENTS WITH LEARNING DISABILITIES

Reading comprehension difficulties are among the most significant problems experienced by children identified with learning disabilities (Kang et al., 2015). A 2001 executive report by the National Reading Panel identified critical skills for reading development: phonemic awareness, phonics, fluency, vocabulary development, and reading comprehension. The report further revealed that a combination of best instructional approaches is most beneficial (National Reading Panel, 2000). Teaching that engages in explicit or direct instruction in phonemic awareness, phonics instruction, guided oral reading, and vocabulary development as well as strategies for reading comprehension are stressed.

Specifically examining reading comprehension, Kim, Linan-Thompson, and Misquitta (2012) divulged five critical components for increasing reading comprehension for students identified as having learning disabilities: using targeted instructional methods, cultivating self-monitoring, combining reading components within an intervention, implementation fidelity, and the size of the instructional group.

Hall (2016) concluded that the most effective inference interventions include instruction in the following areas: activating prior knowledge, integration of prior knowledge into current reading, identification of key words or clues, using key words to answer inferencing questions, and conducting interventions in small groups or one-on-one.

The use of smaller instructional groupings also leads to better student outcomes for those students with reading difficulties; specifically, groups of either one teacher to one student or one teacher to three students have shown greater positive gains than groups of one teacher to ten students or larger (Vaughn & Wanzek, 2014).

Watson and coauthors (2012) compiled a summary of evidenced-based strategies for improving reading comprehension in students with learning disabilities. The most effective evidence-based strategies include activating prior knowledge and explicitly teaching vocabulary, text coherence, and text structure. Peer mentoring and peer-mediated interventions have proven effective increasing reading comprehension in students with learning disabilities as well as in those who simply struggle with comprehension (Kaldenberg, Watt, & Therrien, 2014).

EVIDENCE-BASED WRITING STRATEGIES FOR STUDENTS WITH LEARNING DISABILITIES

The Common Core State Standards place a great deal of emphasis on proficiency in written expression for all learners, including those with disabilities. Proficiency in writing and well-developed writing skills are necessary for students to be successful in college and career readiness (Flanagan & Bouck, 2015; Troia & Olinghouse, 2013). Statistics show that an overwhelming 74 percent of students in grades 8 and 12 are below the proficiency level in writing (Harris & Graham, 2013; NCES, 2012).

The writing process involves complex cognitive, linguistic, affective, and behavioral skills, which must work in harmony (Harris & Graham, 2013; Troia & Olinghouse, 2013). For students with learning disabilities, the writing process can be frustrating and fraught with challenges. Students who experience difficulty developing as readers will most likely struggle with written expression. Students with learning disabilities can experience difficulties in written expression, spelling, grammar, organizing thoughts, and handwriting (Connelly & Dockrell, 2016).

Despite deficits experienced by students with learning disabilities, teachers can support gains through the use of evidence-based writing techniques such as self-regulation strategy development, incorporation of a writing workshop model, and explicit instruction (Harris et al., 2017).

EVIDENCE-BASED MATH STRATEGIES FOR STUDENTS WITH LEARNING DISABILITIES

Approximately 3 to 9 percent of school-aged children are identified as having mathematics disabilities (Watson & Gable, 2013). Students with these disabilities experience difficulties with creating representations, completing mathematical operations, and applying math concepts. According to the Nation's Report Card (2015) an alarming 80 percent of fourth-grade and 92 percent of eighth-grade students with disabilities are at or below basic levels of mathematics proficiency.

One well-researched strategy for supporting students with mathematics disabilities is known as the concrete representational abstract (CRA) framework. The CRA framework is backed by substantial empirical research for teaching many mathematical concepts to students with math disabilities (Agrawal & Morin, 2016; Strickland & Maccini, 2013). This framework assists teachers in guiding students through mathematical concepts using manipulatives, visual representations, and abstract notation (Flores et al., 2014).

Manipulatives within the CRA framework are physical representations that allow students to engage in hands-on learning activities. The visual representations can consist of pictures of manipulatives or virtual manipulatives. These visual manipulatives engage students in the representational phase of learning math concepts (Agrawal & Morin, 2016; Satsangi & Bouck, 2014).

HIGH-QUALITY INSTRUCTIONAL PRACTICES

A vast number of instructional strategies are not considered to be evidence based yet; some of these tend to be extremely beneficial to many students. An instructional strategy may not be labeled evidence based for a number of reasons, including a lack of experimental evidence or a review that has not yet been performed (Council for Exceptional Children, 2014).

Many researchers agree instructional strategies or practices that are not labeled evidence based are not necessarily unsuccessful (Cook & Odom, 2013). These instructional approaches are often referred to as high-quality instructional practices. The best indicator of a high-quality instructional practice is the engagement level of the students with the learning process (Sornson, 2015).

There is substantial evidence supporting the benefits of certain high-quality instructional practices (Sornson, 2015). Several high-quality instructional practices have proven effective for many years, including summarizing and note taking, reinforcing effort and providing recognition, engagement in cooperative learning experiences, goal setting, activating prior knowledge, and creating mental and physical images. These practices were first introduced by Ellis, Worthington, and Larkin (1994) and then expanded upon by Marzano, Pickering, and Pollock (2001) and many others (Sornson, 2015).

EXPOSURE TO EVIDENCE-BASED PRACTICES IN EDUCATOR PREPARATION PROGRAMS

Extensive research supports the legislative requirement for teacher preparation programs to expose preservice teachers to evidence-based instructional practices. The Individuals with Disabilities Education Improvement Act clearly states that teachers need to be trained to identify and implement evidence-based practices (U.S. Department of Education Institute of Education Sciences, National Center for Education Evaluation and Regional Assistance, 2003).

Preservice teachers need to be exposed to evidence-based instructional practices in both theory and practice. This exposure helps teacher candidates to be well-informed practitioners once they are out in the field (Ficarra & Quinn, 2014). But more than exposure, teacher preparation programs must educate preservice teachers on selecting appropriate interventions and practices that are supported by empirical research and being able to implement them with fidelity (Scheeler, Budin, & Markelz, 2016).

Graham and coauthors (2017) believe that fully understanding what evidence-based practices *are* plays a huge role in supporting the conscious decision to choose appropriate strategies to meet the individual learning needs of students. It is well documented that teachers who are well prepared, including extensive instruction in the identification and use of evidence-based practices, are more likely to remain in the field. This ultimately creates stable learning environments that promote positive student outcomes (Ficarra & Quinn, 2014; Kretlow & Helf, 2013).

There are six barriers to the implementation of evidence-based instructional practices: insufficient preparation, lack of reinforcement, competing demands, lack of evidence-based culture, maintenance and generalization, and breadth of expertise (Sheeler, Budin, & Markelz, 2016). A closer examination of these barriers reveals the following insights.

Qualitative surveys of higher education faculty discovered that there is insufficient opportunity for preservice teachers to use evidence-based special education practices in field-based experiences. Teacher preparation programs should incorporate practices that increase preservice teachers' exposure to evidence-based instructional methods. These practices include advanced faculty knowledge and modeling of evidence-based practices within courses, the use of innovative tools, and the use of well-designed clinical experiences out in the field (Scheeler, Budin, & Markelz, 2016).

Faculty knowledge, through engagement in continuous learning, is especially beneficial at creating an atmosphere of awareness of evidence-based practices. Modeling evidence-based instructional strategies within the college classroom supports best practices. Education faculty should focus research efforts on evidence-based practices within all academic areas. Creating a capstone project that engages preservice teachers in actively researching, applying, and evaluating empirically based interventions would be extremely beneficial (Mason-Williams, Frederick, & Mulchay, 2015; Scheeler, Budin, & Markelz, 2016).

EXPOSURE TO EVIDENCE-BASED PRACTICES IN PROFESSIONAL DEVELOPMENT

Many believe that professional development is the link between the goals of educational reform and the implementation and success of the reforms within schools (Demonte, 2013). The Every Student Succeeds Act identified important components of high-quality professional development including those that are research based, focused, aligned with curriculum standards and student learning goals, supportive of school improvement priorities and goals, sustainable within the school environment, and encouraging of collegial relationships (Green & Allen, 2015).

Not only is professional development mandated under federal legislation, it also plays a critical role in supporting and enriching teaching and learning (Green & Allen, 2015). Professional development must be meaningful, relevant, and should focus on research-based pedagogical strategies that support all students in meeting curriculum standards (Bowe & Gore, 2017).

There are several formats for providing professional development opportunities. Well-defined professional learning communities (PLCs) embed learning through collaboration. PLCs are created through common values and visions as well as the belief in shared responsibility for all student learning (Bowe & Gore, 2017). Here the goal is to improve learning through repetitive cycles of inquiry, reflection, and planned change.

Mentoring and coaching provide another opportunity for professional development. Research suggests that teachers who are explicitly taught, guided, and supported through mentoring or coaching partnerships produce positive outcomes in teacher performance and student outcomes (Desimone & Pak, 2017). Mentoring or coaching opportunities can occur one-on-one or within small groups of teachers.

Self-study and action research offer another prospect for engaging in professional development. In action research, an educator identifies an area of concern or focus related to teaching and learning. Benefits of participating in action research efforts include meeting individual professional goals, identifying and addressing individual student learning needs, and engagement in continuous learning (Vanassche & Kelchtermans, 2016).

FINAL THOUGHTS

The implementation of evidence-based instructional practices is required under federal legislation, including the Individuals with Disabilities Education Improvement Act of 2004 and the Every Student Succeeds Act (US Department of Education, 2015a). In addition, extensive research has confirmed the efficacy of evidence-based practices in closing the achievement gap for students with disabilities (Maheady et al., 2016; Scheeler, Budin, & Markelz, 2016). A vast number of evidence-based instructional practices are proven to support students with learning disabilities across various content areas. These include direct and explicit instruction, peer-mediated instruction, application of UDL principles, and self-regulation development strategies (Ford, 2013; Meyer, Rose, & Gordon, 2014; Obiakor et al., 2012; Tomlinson, 2014). There are also a plethora of instructional practices that are not research based that benefit struggling students.

POINTS TO REMEMBER

- *The consistent use of evidence-based instructional strategies is mandated under the Individuals with Disabilities Education Improvement Act of 2004 and the Every Student Succeeds Act of 2015.*
- *Evidence-based instructional practices must be used consistently to help support students with learning disabilities in the least restrictive environment, thereby attempting to close the achievement gap.*
- *High-quality and evidence-based instructional practices must include context and setting, participants, intervention agent, description of practice, implementation fidelity, internal validity and outcome measures, dependent variables, and data analysis.*
- *Extensive exposure to evidence-based instructional practices within teacher preparation programs and professional development opportunities is critical to the successful implementation of said practices.*
- *Teacher training, including professional development opportunities, must focus on research-based pedagogical strategies, including all learning profiles, in meeting curriculum standards.*

Chapter Seven

The Promise of Universal Design for Learning and Assistive Technology

Universal Design for Learning (UDL) is a framework that offers educators a proactive strategy for meeting the needs of all students. The implementation of UDL within the classroom embeds supports, options, and resources prior to instruction (Meyer, Rose, & Gordon, 2014). Created through research in the field of neuroscience and education, UDL identified three principles: multiple means of representation, multiple means of expression, and multiple means of engagement (National Center on Universal Design for Learning, 2017).

The use of assistive technology by students with disabilities enables greater participation by improving access and increasing independence (Center for Parent Information and Resources, 2010). Today, a vast majority of students have access to technology both in and out of the classroom. The use of technology has shown great benefits to the learning of students with disabilities (Ciullo et al., 2015). With the declining cost of various educational technologies, meeting the needs of all students is becoming easier. Both UDL and assistive technology hold great promise for all students, especially those with learning disabilities, as they navigate through their educational careers.

UNIVERSAL DESIGN FOR LEARNING

Universal Design for Learning combines research in the fields of neuroscience and education. The framework allows educators to design learning environments that enhance teaching and learning for all students. UDL is a proactive strategy for integrating supports and choices into the curriculum. UDL plans for the greatest range of needs within the classroom from the beginning; it is not an afterthought (Meyer, Rose, & Gordon, 2014).

The UDL framework consists of three principles: multiple means of representation, multiple means of expression, and multiple means of engagement. In addition, respect for individual differences, learning styles, and personal attributes is embedded throughout the framework (British Columbia Ministry of Education & British Columbia School Superintendent's Association, 2011).

- *Multiple means of representation* ensure that educators provide various options for comprehension, language and math expressions, and perceptions. Examples include activating prior knowledge, highlighting big ideas and vocabulary, customizing the display of information, and emphasizing relationships.
- *Multiple means of expression* provide options for executive functioning, expression and communication, and physical action. Examples include guiding and supporting goal setting, inclusion of multiple tools and media, providing scaffolded supports, and providing various methods for responding.
- *Multiple means of engagement* support motivation for learning by providing options for self-regulation, sustaining effort, and building interest. Examples include setting high expectations, developing self-assessment and self-reflection skills, fostering collaboration and community, and providing individual choice (National Center on Universal Design for Learning, 2017).

CAST is a nonprofit educational and research organization that promotes universal design for learning opportunities in hopes of providing access to all learners (cast.org). CAST has an extensive website offering resources that include webinars, articles, research, videos, and educator tools. The educator tools are completely free and offer a wealth of assistance in planning universally designed lessons, curricula, and assessments. A few of the tools include:

- *UDL Exchange*, a resource that allows educators to create and share instructional materials that are aligned to the Common Core State Standards. Instructional materials across all grade levels and content areas are available.
- *UDL Curriculum Tool Kit*, offering flexible, research-supported curriculum materials for all content areas and grade levels.
- *UDL Studio*, a tool that allows educators to create their own UDL materials with embedded supports and scaffolded opportunities for students.

- *UDL Book Builder*, which allows teachers to create their own interactive digital books.
- *IsolveIt Math*, which incorporates interactive, research-based games and puzzles focused on math reasoning and problem-solving skills.
- *UDL Science Writer*, a web-based scaffolding tool for science content.

ASSISTIVE TECHNOLOGY CONSIDERATIONS IN THE CLASSROOM

Assistive technology devices and services work to assist students with disabilities to participate fully in the least restrictive environment by providing access and promoting independence (Center for Parent Information and Resources, 2010). Assistive technology can support students with learning, socialization, self-care, behavior regulation, and more within all settings to include home, school, and in the community.

According to the Individuals with Disabilities Education Improvement Act (2004), an *assistive technology device* is defined as "any item, piece of equipment, or product system, whether acquired commercially off the shelf, modified, or customized, that is used to increase, maintain, or improve functional capabilities of a child with a disability (National Center for Technology Innovations, 2008, 20 USC 140[1]). Additionally, an *assistive technology service* is defined as "any service that directly assists a child with a disability in the selection, acquisition, or use of an assistive technology device" (20 USC 140[2]).

Any student under the umbrella of special education has the right to access assistive technology supports and services if his or her IEP deems it appropriate if it is included as an accommodation in the IEP (National Center for Technology Innovation, 2008). The consideration of assistive technology devices and services must be discussed when a student becomes eligible for special education. IEP teams must look at the environments in which the student works, the challenges he or she may face, and what the student will require to be successful.

When considering challenges, the IEP should consider such things as handwriting, reading, math, written expression, organization, mobility, seating, self-care, and cognitive processing, among other areas (Center for Parent Information and Resources, 2010). Supplemental technology is being used more often within the traditional classroom. Until now, teachers have been the primary transmitters of information (Bryant et al., 2015). With the increase in educational technology options, the ability to support the learning needs of all students, including those with disabilities, is increasing at an expeditious pace.

Besides the federal mandates, two specific reasons mentioned in the literature support the increased use of technology with students with disabilities. The first is access: Today, more than half of school-aged children have access to some form of technology both in and out of the classroom. The second is that students with disabilities who use computer-assisted technology acknowledge that these tools are critical to their learning (Ciullo et al., 2015). Combined with the rapidly declining cost of such technology, technology offers many options for meeting the needs of students through multiple means of representation, expression, and engagement.

One frequently used type of technology is computer-based instruction, which can assist students in several ways, including offering opportunities for drill and practice, tutorials, participation in academic games, problem-solving, and computer-managed instruction (Bryant et al., 2015). There are newer computer-based instructional programs created specifically for mobile devices such as phones and tablets. Research has supported the effectiveness of computer-based instruction in enhancing the functional capabilities of students with disabilities (Bryant et al., 2015; Bryant & Bryant, 2011).

There are numerous advantages to mobile instructional applications, including access to inexpensive, easily downloadable programs, the use of touch screens, portability due to small device sizes and longer battery life, the ability to connect to the Internet, and access to built-in accessibility functions (Bryant et al., 2015; Ok et al., 2016).

Graphic organizers are assistive tools that help students organize information in order to understand concepts. Graphic organizers help to empower students to become engaged learners. In relation to increasing reading comprehension, Watson and coauthors (2012) describe graphic organizers as providing students with "a cognitive structure, a framework to relate existing knowledge to new information to be learned" (p. 83). The use of graphic organizers provides students with a conceptual image of what it is they are reading or learning.

The use of graphic organizers can play a role in activating a learner's schema and assist with connecting ideas. The use of graphic organizers allows for the quick retrieval of information or reading elements to assist with comprehension and prevents overloading working memory. By decreasing such overload, students are able to better use their cognitive resources to comprehend and make connections.

Several computer applications provide students with interactive graphic organizers, including concept maps. Programs such as Kidspiration (Inspiration Software, 2017) allow students to design and customize their own graphic organizers to fit all content areas (Ciullo et al., 2015).

Funding for Assistive Technology

While the costs are declining, assistive technology devices can be expensive. When a child in special education is identified as requiring the aid of assistive technology support and services, the local educational agency is obligated by federal regulation to provide it (National Center for Technology Innovation, 2008). As funding means are often scare, it behooves school districts and families to work together to identify alternative sources such as:

- *Private Funding Sources.* Private funding sources include charitable organizations and other 501(c)(3) organizations. The Knights of Columbus, Rotary Clubs, and Lions Clubs are examples of civic organizations that have provided funding for assistive technology for students.
- *ADA Technical Assistance Programs.* Under the Americans with Disabilities Act, each state has an ADA Technical Assistance program that can provide numerous benefits including funding, training, and support for assistive technology resources.
- *Health Insurance Programs.* Sometimes school districts will ask families to access their own health-care coverage as a means of funding the purchase of assistive technology equipment. When looking into this avenue, it is important to make sure that it does not put a financial burden on the family.
- *Lending Libraries and Used Equipment Options.* Many disability-related organizations offer schools the opportunity to borrow assistive technology equipment. Many of these lending libraries such as the Regional Disability and Business Technical Assistance Center and the Assistive Technology Network, may be found on the Internet.
- *Used Equipment Marketplace.* Individuals can buy and sell assistive technology equipment. Some examples of used equipment marketplaces include Access Technologies, Inc.; the NEAT Center at Oak Hill; and the Wisconsin Assistive Technology Initiative.
- *Online Resources for Educators.* Online resources provide information on available grants, databases of various assistive technology equipment, and how to buy assistive technology equipment in bulk. Examples of these online resources include Maryland Assistive Technology Cooperative, the Infinitetec of Illinois, EdTechOnline.org, and TechMatrix.org (National Center for Technology Innovation, 2008).

FINAL THOUGHTS

Universal Design for Learning combines knowledge about how the brain learns (neuroscience) with educational research to meet the needs of all students. The implementation of UDL within the classroom provides multiple means of representation, expression, and engagement (Meyer, Rose, & Gordon, 2014; National Center on Universal Design for Learning, 2017). Rooted in the principles of UDL are student choices, acceptance of learning styles, supports, and technological resources.

In addition to the use of UDL, the incorporation of assistive technology by students with disabilities improves access to learning, increases independence, and ensures academic gains (Center for Parent Information and Resources, 2010). Technology is becoming a popular fixture within today's classrooms. Educational applications and computer-based instruction have proven effective at meeting diverse student needs (Ciullo et al., 2015).

POINTS TO REMEMBER

- *Universal Design for Learning incorporates extensive neuroscience research with educational research to provide the best possible solutions for addressing the learning needs of diverse learners.*
- *UDL provides students with choices, supports, and resources that relate to their preferred learning modality.*
- *Assistive technology supports students with disabilities in accessing the learning environment, promoting socialization, and increasing independence.*
- *Technology use in the classroom is universally increasing and providing students with additional ways to obtain information, comprehend what they are learning, and expand their knowledge base.*
- *Together, UDL and assistive technology become a type of personalized learning that all educators can offer to their students with learning disabilities.*

Chapter Eight

Working with Paraprofessionals

Best Practices for Supporting and Training

There has been an increase in the number of paraprofessionals in the educational field, particularly within special education classrooms, where they have become an integral component assisting students with learning disabilities (Brock, 2015). Teacher shortages and rising enrollment of students with disabilities and other special needs make paraprofessionals within the classroom critically necessary for improving student achievement (National Education Association, 2015).

QUALIFICATIONS

Federal laws such as the Individuals with Disabilities Education Act of 1990 allow appropriately trained and supervised paraprofessionals to assist in the provision of special education to students with disabilities (Biggs, Gilson, & Carter, 2016). Under the Every Student Succeeds Act of 2015, a paraprofessional working alongside an educator in the classroom must have a secondary school diploma and have completed a minimum of two years of study in higher education.

Paraprofessionals must also demonstrate, on a formal state or local academic assessment, that he or she has the knowledge and ability to assist in instructing educational topics such as reading, writing, and arithmetic (Connecticut State Department of Education, 2012). A paraprofessional working in a classroom may provide instructional services to students only under the direct supervision of a licensed teacher, and may not remain in the classroom alone with students (Masters in Education Program Guide, 2017b).

RESPONSIBILITIES

The National Resource Center for Paraeducators (NRCP) model framework defines six primary areas of responsibility for paraprofessionals in working with educators in the classroom. These areas include assisting teachers with building and maintaining effective instructional teams, supporting teachers with planning, organizing learning experiences, maintaining learner-centered supportive environments, assessing student learning needs, and assisting the classroom teacher in student engagement through instruction that helps educators assess the progress and achievement of students (Connecticut State Department of Education, 2012).

Other paraprofessional responsibilities may include the provision of one-on-one tutoring and translating, assisting with classroom management, and conducting parental involvement activities (Klein, 2015). In addition, paraprofessionals can assist in ensuring that the national standards of professional and ethical conduct are upheld for each of these responsibilities (Connecticut State Department of Education, 2012).

The US Department of Education states that paraprofessionals may provide instructional support to students but cannot provide direct instruction or introduce students to new skills, concepts, or academic content. Paraprofessionals can provide instruction that is not new to the class if they have been appropriately trained and are under the direct supervision of a certified teacher (Connecticut State Department of Education, 2012).

It is necessary that those paraprofessionals who support students with disabilities have access to and an understanding of the students' IEPs. Familiarity with a student's IEP and the services provided therein will help the paraprofessional to understand his or her role in implementing the IEP (Connecticut State Department of Education, 2012).

A basic understanding of a student's disabilities may be helpful to a paraprofessional's interaction and work with a student. For example, knowing the characteristics of the most common disabilities found within the classroom may help paraprofessionals be better prepared for challenging situations and help understand their strengths. There may be occasions when a paraprofessional needs very specific information about a student and his or her particular disability in order to work more effectively with the student. In these situations, it is important that more specific training for both the teacher and the paraprofessional be available (Connecticut State Department of Education, 2012).

THE RELATIONSHIP BETWEEN SPECIAL
EDUCATOR AND PARAPROFESSIONAL

Supervision

Paraprofessionals provide instructional support, including one-on-one tutoring to students with disabilities, under the direct supervision of the educator within the classroom (US Department of Education, 2016). Achievement outcomes are increased when an educator prepares lesson plans that guide the paraprofessional in supportive work with the student (Connecticut State Department of Education, 2012).

According to French (n.d.), key factors in providing adequate supervision to paraprofessionals are akin to the executive functions performed by business team leaders. As such, educators are responsible for orienting new paraprofessionals to the classroom, setting a schedule, and creating specific job descriptions. Delegating responsibilities, providing plans and directions for delegated work, and monitoring a paraprofessional's performance to ensure the work is completed sufficiently also fall within an educator's purview.

Paraprofessionals who work with children who have disabilities in a general education classroom might spend the majority of the day out of the direct supervision of the special education teacher and can therefore be missing adequate support and supervision (Alquarini & Gut, 2012). When this occurs, a more collaborative model of supervision can be used in which teachers encourage paraprofessionals to engage in independent reflection and goal setting (Douglas, Chapin, & Nolan, 2016).

In one study (Douglas, Chapin, & Nolan, 2016) researchers examined the practices of multiple teachers who were nominated as outstanding supervisors of paraprofessionals to understand key elements and methods that could be utilized to ensure students with learning disabilities were supported in the classroom. Through interviews, the authors discovered that educators had many positive experiences when working with paraprofessionals, including positive team relationships that were accomplished through teamwork, shared responsibilities, mutual respect, and good communication. When asked about training opportunities for working with paraprofessionals and acquired supervisory skills, many educators indicated that they were provided little or no training. It appears that more training was available for paraprofessionals to work with educators than the other way around.

As demonstrated through these interviews, teachers received very little formal training on working with and supervising paraprofessionals, yet paraprofessional training included formal group training that met district and state requirements. Formal training was provided by the district or state educational agencies and consisted of training on data collection, CPR/first aid, autism, academic topics, and inclusion (Douglas, Chapin, & Nolan, 2016).

Paraprofessionals who were interviewed also received the majority of their training informally from special education teachers, although occasional training was conducted by behavior specialists and school psychologists (Douglas, Chapin, & Nolan, 2016). It is vital that both paraprofessionals and educators receive training on working cooperatively.

Teamwork

Developing effective professional working relationships among teachers and paraprofessionals is essential to providing students with high-quality educational experiences. Effective and collaborative teamwork is also essential for students with disabilities who have an extra need for support and in providing quality educational programs (Biggs, Gilson, & Carter, 2016).

In order to foster a successful working relationship and make sure the classroom runs smoothly, educators and paraprofessionals should strive to maintain effective communication, create problem-solving strategies, and mediate inconsistencies using agreed-upon conflict management approaches. To ensure successful performance within the classroom, educators should provide paraprofessionals with defined roles and responsibilities, constructive feedback on performance, coaching when necessary, and opportunities for appropriate training and professional development (French, n.d.).

A study by Biggs, Gilson, and Carter (2016) looked at the factors influencing the quality of relationships between special education teachers and paraprofessionals through a series of questionnaires and interviews that addressed various characteristics of professional roles and responsibilities. Participants were recruited from three school districts serving urban, suburban, and rural communities and included a mixture of those working in public schools, integrated schools, and community-based transition programs affiliated with public high schools.

The study found that positive relationships were formed between dedicated teachers and paraprofessionals when educators were open, understanding, confident, and flexible, while staying focused on the students. Paraprofessionals described significant qualities that contributed to teacher job effectiveness as organization, teaching skills, educational knowledge, and professionalism (Biggs, Gilson, & Carter, 2016).

Paraprofessionals appreciated when educators set expectations; they valued clear and explicit communication regarding information on classroom tasks that was necessary to success in their roles. The relationship between the teacher and paraprofessional felt more like a team when teachers considered the strengths of paraprofessionals in making decisions that affected the classroom (Biggs, Gilson, & Carter, 2016).

Although educators valued paraprofessionals' skills and knowledge, they did point out that because paraprofessionals had such varied backgrounds, minimal preservice training, and limited professional development, they did not feel the paraprofessionals were fully equipped for their responsibilities. Paraprofessional proficiency was demonstrated by a willingness and/or eagerness to learn and when a paraprofessional took an active role within the classroom by asking questions, seeking help, or pursuing professional development opportunities (Biggs, Gilson, & Carter, 2016).

Although teachers said that providing feedback to paraprofessionals on their work was challenging and felt confrontational, paraprofessionals valued teachers' ability to provide honest, frequent, and constructive feedback. The relationship between teachers and paraprofessionals was negatively affected when performance was not discussed or when, instead of being constructive and supportive, the paraprofessional felt the feedback was critical or judgmental (Biggs, Gilson, & Carter, 2016).

The teacher-paraprofessional relationship was positively impacted when, according to study participants, the paraprofessionals filled unmet needs within the classroom and provided valuable feedback and/or encouragement (Biggs, Gilson, & Carter, 2016).

According to the respondents, some of the most important qualities for a successful teacher-paraprofessional relationship that promotes student success within the classroom include mutual respect, shared long-term visions for the classroom, investment in the same goals, and similar expectations for students. According to both teachers and paraprofessionals, mutual respect means that both parties should demonstrate a positive, caring attitude toward students; be dependable, prompt, and reliable; assist each other without being asked; and value each other's contribution (Biggs, Gilson, & Carter, 2016).

TRAINING AND SUPPORT OF PARAPROFESSIONALS

Studies suggest that without strong and adequate training, paraprofessional presence and support in the classroom does not appear to improve the learning outcomes of students with disabilities, and may actually hinder them (Brock, 2015). The American Federation of Teachers (AFT) promotes and encourages professional development for paraprofessionals by providing boards of education with training modules and curricula, and developing strategies to improve communication between teachers and paraprofessionals (Connecticut State Department of Education, 2012).

AFT offers various training programs, including role-playing and team-building exercises, that help define and improve the teacher-paraprofessional relationship and create an environment of professional cooperation (Connecticut State Department of Education, 2012). Effective training programs should clearly communicate how to implement educational interventions (modeling), ensure participants are successful in their attempt to implement the intervention (accountability), and follow-up through performance feedback to reinforce successes and help in areas that need improvement (Brock, 2015).

Single-event trainings and workshops, also known as *faculty in-services*, are the most common school-based professional development opportunity—even though they may be ineffective at furnishing paraprofessionals with the necessary knowledge and information to deliver high-quality instructional support. Instead of depending solely on stand-alone training workshops, special education teachers might consider scheduling follow-up training periods and coaching sessions throughout the year to provide more focused support and evaluate paraprofessional performance (Brock, 2015).

In a study by Brock (2015), modeling, accountability, and performance feedback were combined into a flexible and replicable training package called Video Modeling Plus Abbreviated Coaching (VMPAC). VMPAC involved an initial training workshop followed by video modeling and abbreviated on-site coaching. In a randomized controlled trial of twenty-five paraprofessionals who served children with disabilities, Brock (2015) found that the follow-up training package was effective and that coaching was the most powerful component. Training opportunities that promoted acquisition of practitioner knowledge, yet failed to demonstrate how educators provided instruction in the classroom, were of little benefit to students with disabilities. The findings from this study have implications for public school administrators and special education professionals who make decisions on equipping and supervising paraprofessionals.

IDEA (IDEA Partnership, n.d.) stipulates that paraprofessionals who are appropriately trained and supervised may assist teachers in the provision of special education and related services; however, IDEA does not provide any guidance on what constitutes *appropriate* training and supervision (Brock, 2015).

EVIDENCE-BASED INSTRUCTIONAL PRACTICES

Considering the lack of certification and education, varying levels of experience, and the diverse and considerable needs of the population they serve, paraprofessionals are likely to benefit from the provision of additional resources and training regarding the use of evidence-based instructional practices (EBIPs). Increasing the implementation and use of EBIPs through modeling and coaching, particularly in special education, can increase student engagement and learning opportunities and decrease the amount of time spent in ineffective education, which can result in improved student outcomes. EBIPs should embrace effective teaching of academic and social skills as well as appropriate responses to insolent behavior that result in less than desirable student outcomes (Ledford et al., 2017).

Ledford and coauthors (2017) focused their research on EBIPs and coaching procedures for improving the instructional practices of paraprofessionals. As part of their study, three paraprofessional-student teams participated in didactic training sessions in which modeling with classroom materials was coupled with information and sample videos.

The results of this study demonstrate changes in academic and social behavior, such as answering questions and reading sight words, among students. Changes also occurred in paraprofessional behavior for those who had limited knowledge and skill in teaching students with disabilities (Ledford et al., 2017).

Direct Instruction Training

The direct instruction training model (DITM) consists of six steps that are performed by the teacher: establishing training goals and objectives to be carried out by the paraprofessional, instructing, demonstrating, guiding, observing the paraprofessional, and providing performance feedback. While the teacher is performing these objectives, the paraprofessional listens, responds, questions, practices, and self-evaluates after each lesson (Stockall, 2014).

A variety of staff development and training paradigms can enhance the performance of paraprofessionals. Pairing paraprofessionals with licensed teachers in ongoing professional development may ensure the achievement of certain competencies (Connecticut State Department of Education, 2012).

Skill development training can also take place within the instructional setting, where educators might model or coach paraprofessionals while working directly with students. Some of the most effective training can take place in team meetings when teams work collaboratively on problem solving and strategies (Connecticut State Department of Education, 2012).

THE BENEFIT OF PARAPROFESSIONALS

In 2013, 96 percent of the 416,798 special education paraprofessionals who provided special education and related services under IDEA were qualified to do so, yet this has been the subject of continued debate (Masters in Education Program Guide, 2017b). Paraprofessionals can be valuable members of an educational community and can offer students many benefits—provided they have the proper training and support. As Goe and Matlach (2014) point out, the use of paraprofessionals in the classroom may allow teachers to spend more time with individual students in small groups and facilitate school-family and school-community relationships.

It is critical to evaluate a student's needs, particularly when that student works one-on-one with a paraprofessional, to determine if the assistance of the paraprofessional is actually beneficial to the student. Research has shown that effective targeting of academic and social skills and the minimization of problem behavior that results from working with a paraprofessional can lead to improved student learning outcomes, both short- and long-term and in other educational settings. When students receive more effective instruction, they may be less likely to need frequent assistance (Ledford et al., 2017).

It is important to consider the possibility that a student might need less assistance, as other research has shown that having a paraprofessional constantly by a student's side can interfere with classroom experiences and inclusion in the classroom community, resulting in fewer peer interactions and increased stereotyping (Ledford et al., 2017). Studies also suggest that without strong training, paraprofessional support does not appear to improve students' learning outcomes (Brock, 2015).

Contrary to the widespread belief that paraprofessionals are essential, Blatchford, Russell, and Webster (2012) reported few, if any, positive outcomes for students working with paraprofessionals (Stockall, 2014). In fact, the use of paraprofessionals can inadvertently cause a student to separate from the classroom and to depend on the paraprofessional, interfering in relationships with peers. Students working with paraprofessionals may have limited access to professionally trained and certified educators and may lose already established relationships with their teachers (Jericho School District, 2017; Wang, 2013).

According to a study by Wang (2013), the use of paraprofessionals with students who have learning disabilities can lead to many disadvantages, including the fact that complex educational decisions may be made by noncertified teachers. Another concern is that students may be labeled as disabled, lose their independence, and have increased behavioral problems simply because they are assisted by a paraprofessional.

FINAL THOUGHTS

The increasing number of paraprofessionals that are necessary to work within special education to improve student achievement can be attributed to the rising enrollment of students with disabilities. Under law, paraprofessionals may assist within the classroom as long as they are appropriately trained, have a secondary school diploma, and are under the direct supervision of a certified teacher (US Department of Education, 2015a; IDEA Partnership, n.d.).

In order to support students with disabilities effectively, paraprofessionals should have an understanding of a student's IEP and the services it provides to the student. Familiarity with the common characteristics of a student's disability may also be helpful in the interaction between the paraprofessional and the student. School administration should provide training opportunities to paraprofessionals to help them understand the specific details of particular disabilities.

Professional development for paraprofessionals is encouraged and provided in areas such as the development of strategies to improve communication between paraprofessionals and teachers. These trainings, which may take the form of training programs or role-playing and team-building exercises, aim to help define and improve teacher-paraprofessional relationships and cooperation.

Paraprofessionals who work with disabled children in a general education classroom may be out of the direct supervision of the special education teacher and may therefore lack adequate support and supervision (Alquarini & Gut, 2012). Research has discovered that supportive methods within positive teacher-paraprofessional relationships such as shared responsibilities, mutual respect, and good communication can ensure appropriate supervision occurs (Douglas, Chapin, & Nolan, 2016).

Much debate has recently ensued regarding whether paraprofessionals in the classroom are actually of benefit to students. Research has shown that students who work with paraprofessionals have improved learning outcomes and superior long-term outcomes in later educational settings, yet students may be stereotyped, labeled, separated from their teacher and peers (Ledford et al., 2017).

POINTS TO REMEMBER

- *The Individuals with Disabilities Education Act of 1990 allows appropriately trained and supervised paraprofessionals to assist in the provision of special education of students with disabilities. Paraprofessionals must be under the direct supervision of the teacher and cannot be left alone in the classroom with the students.*
- *Paraprofessionals can ensure that the national standards of professional and ethical conduct are complied with for each of their classroom responsibilities. These responsibilities can include supporting teachers with planning and maintaining learner-centered supportive environments, one-on-one tutoring, classroom management, and assessing student learning needs (Connecticut State Department of Education, 2012).*
- *Without strong and adequate training, paraprofessional support in the classroom may not improve student learning outcomes and may actually hinder them. Training can take place within the classroom, but the most*

effective training takes place in team meetings where the team can work collaboratively.

- *Effective teacher-paraprofessional relationships are essential to providing students with high-quality educational experiences and attaining successful learning outcomes. Important qualities that teachers and paraprofessionals should share in their relationship include mutual respect, shared long-term visions, investment in the same goals, and similar expectations for students (Biggs, Gilson, & Carter, 2016).*
- *Although paraprofessionals are essential, in some circumstances they may be doing the student a disservice. It is of concern that a student may be labeled and stereotyped as a result of working with a paraprofessional.*

Chapter Nine

Providing Educator Support through Professional Development

According to the Every Student Succeeds Act of 2015, professional development is needed in order to retain effective teachers, improve methods of instruction, and efficiently use data from academic assessments performed within school systems. To be effective and successful, professional development programs must be first-rate and relevant to the teachers' needs and work environments, and must include training on mentoring, teamwork, observation, reflection, and assessment (Burns, 2011; Connecticut State Department of Education, 2012).

According to Burns (2011), professional development should focus on helping teachers develop knowledge, skills, and attitudes that will enhance teaching as well as expand their content knowledge and pedagogical skills. Training should also model the exact behavioral goals teachers should exhibit in the classroom and include opportunities for practice and reflection.

In order to make professional development more attainable for educators, information and training related to student learning should be embedded within the work day and sustained over time. A sense of collegiality and collaboration should be developed among teachers and between teachers and administration to solve problems related to teaching and learning. The creation and existence of professional learning communities can also provide technical and social support as well as develop and enhance teacher leadership skills (Burns, 2011).

EFFECTIVE PROFESSIONAL DEVELOPMENT

Effective professional development focuses on teaching strategies associated with specific curriculum content and supports teacher learning within the context of the classroom. In addition, high-quality professional development supports collaboration by creating time and space for teachers to share ideas and collaborate in their learning. By working together, teachers can create educational communities that make positive changes in culture and instruction, starting with their grade level and working all the way up to the entire school and/or district (Darling-Hammond, Hyler, & Gardner, 2017).

Successful professional development uses effective models of practice regarding curriculum and instruction in order to provide teachers with a clear vision of best practices. Coaching and expert support give the opportunity for direct focus on individual teacher needs and involve the sharing of expertise about content and evidence-based practices (Darling-Hammond, Hyler, & Gardner, 2017).

Best practice professional development strategies provide built-in time over a sustained duration for teachers to reflect, receive feedback, and make changes to their instructional methods. Effective training also moves away from traditional lecture-based learning models and has no direct connection to teachers' classrooms and students (Darling-Hammond, Hyler, & Gardner, 2017).

Professional learning is one of the strongest ways to increase student achievement. While student achievement expectations are rising, the more diverse student population has made it essential that students receive effective teaching in order to develop the higher-order thinking skills necessary to enter postsecondary education or to enter the workforce (Generation Ready, 2013).

Professional development is a comprehensive, continuous, and concentrated approach to improving teachers' effectiveness in raising student achievement. Effective professional development can guide improvement and measure impact through evidence-based practices and data gathered from the school. Training is rigorous and embedded within the context of the school and classroom in order to ensure an intense focus on the teacher-learner relationship. The data and information gathered can be used to foster collaborative school relationships and provide a measurable link to school achievement goals (Generation Ready, 2013).

TEACHER-CENTERED PROFESSIONAL DEVELOPMENT MODEL

It has been found that professional development models that include coaching and mentoring, study groups, lesson study, and observation and assessment are more effective than workshops or trainings (Burns, 2011). Teacher-centered professional development models may be used as a form of peer coaching to support educators throughout the academic year (Burns, 2014).

Teaching Styles

Professional development is a career-long process in which educators develop and expand their teaching to meet the changing needs of students. According to Diaz-Maggioli (2017), a teacher's style of instruction is a subtle force that influences students' access to learning. Each educator has his or her own particular teaching style that can range from student-centered to teacher-centered and that always affects classroom performance.

The Teacher's Choice Framework

Creators of professional development programs should keep in mind that teachers are talented individuals who possess a vast amount of experience and a treasure trove of knowledge to explore. The theoretical and professional knowledge teachers have gained in the classroom can offer a wealth of resources and knowledge that can be shared (Diaz-Maggioli, 2017). Educators, administrators, and counselors, virtually anyone who works with students during the school day, should include quality professional development daily and consider it a career-long investment in contributing to student success (Diaz-Maggioli, 2017).

Professional development and knowledge about teaching and learning will advance student learning outcomes only if it involves the whole school community and is in the context of the school's culture and climate. To ensure professional development activities are successful and productive, educators need an organizational framework based on individual characteristics and personal contributions (Diaz-Maggioli, 2017).

The Teacher's Choice Framework assists teachers in making individual and joint decisions by collaboratively reflecting on student learning data. Data should be gathered and shared across all grades and disciplines so that a professional development program can be designed that addresses the needs of all stakeholders (Diaz-Maggioli, 2017).

Cascade Model of Professional Development

In the cascade model of professional development, training occurs at multiple levels and is disseminated throughout the lower levels of a system. Within the educational field this means that one or two teachers attend a centralized training to build upon their current skills and learn new skills. At the conclusion of the training, those teachers then return to their school district to share what they have learned with their colleagues (Fulton et al., 2012).

This type of flexible training is most effective when focused on small-group interactions customized for each district's needs, and used with detailed training manuals, organized and meaningful presentations, and resources such as websites and/or videos (Fulton et al., 2012). One of the main benefits associated with the cascade model of training is its cost effectiveness: One person from a school might attend a training and is then expected to return to the school district and provide training to many others. This method of instruction provides for a rapid dissemination of information on specific skills and content and allows many teachers to be trained at the same time, thereby reducing cost (Bett, 2016). The success of cascade training depends on the quality of the trainers.

Research has also demonstrated disadvantages to this type of model. The information present at the training can become diluted, and what one participant hears may be different than the intention of the original message. One inherent risk is that less information is passed on to each successive level. In this model teachers may not be selecting what they learn, and the information presented may be irrelevant to the teacher and to the needs of the school (Fulton et al., 2012; Bett, 2016).

One key characteristic of the cascade model is that trainings are often held in settings other than the school environment; this eventually becomes disadvantageous, as the training grounds vary from the school setting and context. As a result, on many occasions teachers fail to link training to context and end up experiencing challenges in applying information from the training to their work in the classroom (Fulton et al., 2012).

Learner-Centered Professional Development

In the learner-centered professional development model, teachers design, examine, and reflect on, the same style of learning they will share with their students (Darling-Hammond, Hyler, & Gardner, 2017). This type of training is central to continuous learning in that it allows educators to use feedback and reflection to deepen their knowledge and skills (eTools4Education, 2017).

In the same way that personalized learning works for students, learner-centered professional development requires teachers to participate in their own learning by identifying what they need to learn and working collaboratively to gain the skills necessary to master their selected content. Selected content should center on what students need to learn, and particularly on those fundamentals that students have the most difficulty learning. The substance of this training is determined by analyzing discrepancies between learning outcomes/actual student performance and student learning standards and goals (Hanover Research, 2013).

Professional development using this model should focus on identified instructional goals in subject matter areas established by the learning needs of the student population (Hanover Research, 2013). Recognized challenges associated with learner-centered training include establishing consistency and lack of buy-in from school administration and teachers themselves (eTools4Education, 2017).

Self-Directed Professional Development

All professional development should be self-directed, as individual teachers should have the independence to choose what training best suits their personal learning styles. Research has found that the most effective professional development takes place when teachers are in control of their own learning. Self-directed professional development opens the door for teachers to learn in any place and at any time, allowing them to access a wide variety of skills and training outside the classroom at their own pace (British Columbia Teachers Federation, 2017).

Through self-directed professional development, educators have the opportunity to become involved in ongoing self-directed learning and to spend time collaborating with specifically chosen colleagues. Teachers can work in teams on projects they believe to be significant in the context of their school culture and share their knowledge and resources with other team members. Discussions among professionals give teachers the opportunity to strengthen their instructional methods of practice and to evaluate teaching styles and leadership through research (Miyata, 2016).

Self-directed professional development is beneficial to educators, providing access to quality instructional materials akin to training from master teachers or high-quality instructional coaches. Educators can review difficult concepts and gain mastery of those topics without fear of a set time limit (Rethink, 2017).

Self-directed training can also solve challenges associated with integrated co-teaching, and teachers can learn highly effective techniques to strengthen inclusion classrooms. Paraprofessionals who work with students with disabilities, who may have once been excluded from professional development opportunities provided to certified teachers, now have access to those same opportunities. Other related service providers can discover new and inventive ways to help students with special or social/behavioral needs (Rethink, 2017).

IMPLICATIONS FOR POLICY AND PRACTICE

Successful professional development programs that result in increased student achievement can help policy makers and practitioners to better understand what quality teaching and successful learning looks like. According to a 2017 report by the Learning Policy Institute, policy makers should adopt standards for professional development to direct the design, evaluation, and funding of professional learning provided to educators (Darling-Hammond, Hyler, & Gardner, 2017).

Policy makers should also regularly conduct needs assessments to identify the areas of professional learning that are needed and desired by educators. This data can help ensure that professional learning is connected with practice and supports the areas of knowledge and skills educators want to develop (Darling-Hammond, Hyler, & Gardner, 2017).

To facilitate professional development, school administrators should evaluate and redesign the use of school time to increase opportunities for learning and collaboration, including participation in coaching, observations across classrooms, and collaborative planning. Expert teachers should be identified as mentors and coaches to support learning in their area(s) of expertise. School administrators and districts should bestow flexible funding for learning opportunities that include sustained engagement in collaboration, mentoring, and coaching, as well as institutes, workshops, and seminars (Darling-Hammond, Hyler, & Gardner, 2017).

Well-designed and well-thought-out professional development should be implemented as an essential component of an all-encompassing system of teaching and learning that supports students in developing the knowledge, skills, and competencies they need to succeed. To ensure a consistent system that supports all educators, professional learning should link to classroom experiences and teaching standards (Darling-Hammond, Hyler, & Gardner, 2017).

AVAILABLE SOURCES FOR PROFESSIONAL DEVELOPMENT OPPORTUNITIES

Today, the roles and functions of schools and the duties and responsibilities placed upon educators continue to change. Educators are often asked to help students succeed in the midst of challenges such as growing class sizes, new tests, new rules, and new evaluation measures (Rethink, 2017). During this time of increasing change, educators must choose appropriate resources to help prepare for upcoming career challenges.

Effective professional development provides educators with meaningful training through active engagement, thus allowing the quality of classroom instruction to improve and transform while the educator grows professionally and strengthens his or her practice (Rethink, 2017).

The National Staff Development Council Standards for Professional Development (Learning Forward, 2015) reflect the most current best practices in professional learning. The standards examine what students are expected to know and do, what teachers must do to ensure student success, and what methods professional development must use to meet both goals.

The Library of Congress offers a series of professional development opportunities to educational organizations and teachers that explains the "rich reservoir of digitized primary source materials [available] to design challenging, high-quality instruction" (Library of Congress, n.d.). Professional development content includes activities such as ready-to-present models, interactive self-directed video modules, and videos on using resources and teaching strategies for using primary sources within the classroom.

The National Archives (2017) provides educators the opportunity to participate in document-based workshops where they learn how to find and teach using primary sources and specific historical topics. The National Archives also provides online/distance learning through professional development webinars, recorded programs, and trainings on YouTube and National History Day workshops.

The National Education Association (NEA) believes that professional development should be required for paraprofessionals throughout their careers and that training should provide equal opportunities for paraprofessionals to gain and improve their knowledge and skills. The NEA (2015) states that student achievement depends on supporting and educating the whole student and that in order to meet the high standards set for students, there must also be high standards for the educators who work with them.

The NEA offers a wide variety of professional development programs through its state affiliates, including professional development opportunities such as the NEA Education Support Professional (ESP) National Conference and the NEA ESP Leaders for Tomorrow program. Both conferences seek to help paraprofessionals gain the skills they need to build strong internal and external relationships and positively influence student achievement (NEA, 2015).

The Council for Exceptional Children professional development services team creates ongoing professional learning opportunities for special educators and other support personnel who instruct and support children with disabilities. CEC's professional training relates to the current issues and trends in education using formats that educators use every day (CEC, 2017).

FINAL THOUGHTS

Effective professional development allows educators to increase their knowledge and skills to work effectively with students and improve learning outcomes. To be successful, professional development programs must be relevant to the needs of the teachers and their students and include training on mentoring, teamwork, observation, reflection, and assessment (Burns, 2011; Connecticut Department of Education, 2012). Professional development should be content focused, support teacher learning, and provide time for teachers to share ideas and collaborate in order to create educational communities that make positive changes in culture and instruction.

Professional development models that include coaching, mentoring, observation, and assessment are more effective than standard workshops and training (Burns, 2011). Active learning provides teachers with the opportunity to participate in the same style of learning they design for their students and is central to school improvement (Darling-Hammond, Hyler, & Gardner, 2017; eTools4Education, 2017). All professional development should be self-directed and put teachers in control of their own learning by offering the independent choice regarding what training is best suited for their individual learning styles (British Columbia Teachers Federation, 2017).

Successful professional development programs that increase student achievement can assist policy makers in understanding quality teaching and successful learning. Policy makers should adopt standards for professional development and regularly conduct needs assessments to identify the desired areas of professional learning and connect learning to practice and support to knowledge and skills (Darling-Hammond, Hyler, & Gardner, 2017).

POINTS TO REMEMBER

- *Professional development should model the exact behavioral goals to be exhibited by teachers in the classroom and include opportunities for practice and reflection (Burns, 2011). To make professional development more accessible to educators, information and training related to student learning should be rooted within the work day (Burns, 2011).*
- *Professional development is a comprehensive, continuous, and concentrated approach used to improve teachers' effectiveness in fostering student success and can be used to promote collaborative school relationships and measurable links to school achievement.*
- *Cascade model training is most effective when focused on small groups, customized for individual district needs, and used with detailed training manuals, meaningful presentations, and electronic resources (Fulton et al., 2012). A few of the main benefits associated with this style of professional development are its cost effectiveness, rapid dissemination of information, and the ability to train many teachers simultaneously.*
- *Self-directed promotional development can solve challenges associated with integrated co-teaching and provide teachers with techniques to strengthen inclusion classrooms. Under this training model, paraprofes-*

sionals have the opportunity to participate in professional development that was previously available only to certified teachers (Rethink, 2017).

Chapter Ten

Postsecondary Education

How to Support a Smooth Transition from Secondary to Higher Education for Students with Disabilities

The Individuals with Disabilities Education Improvement Act of 2004 (IDEIA Partnership, n.d.) charges students with disabilities to be engaged and proactive in developing transition plans for college and the long-term planning of their future. When planning for the transition from high school to an institute of higher education, students, parents, and special education team members must base the goals of the plan on the student's strengths, preferences, interests, and needs (US Department of Education, 2007).

Transition planning forms must include student goals for after graduating with a regular high school diploma or attaining the age of twenty-two. Student IEPs must include measurable postsecondary transition goals, objectives, and services based upon a proper evaluation of the student's disability and transition needs (US Department of Education, 2007).

While in secondary education a student's parents played a significant role in advocating for his or her learning needs, with the student's shift into college, the parents' advocacy role also shifts from their shoulders onto the student's (Young, Michael, & Citro, 2017). Positive parent involvement and support is always welcome at the collegiate level; however, overinvolvement is a disservice to the student, who now needs to be more independent and assume the responsibilities of self-advocacy.

Parents who take advocating for their child to the extreme and become helicopter parents prevent their children from learning self-advocacy skills and gaining the confidence they will need throughout their academic careers and beyond. In some instances, the Family Educational Rights and Privacy Act may even prevent parents from taking an active role in their student's involvement with college disability service departments (US Department of Education, 2015b).

It is beneficial to the student if those parents who want to stay involved with their student's education do so at an appropriate level that facilitates student success. Students whose parents collaborate with them, instead of directing and controlling them, to solve problems and find access to important resources tend to experience a smoother transition into college (Young, Michael, & Citro, 2017).

SELF-DISCLOSURE

Many students leave high school lacking self-awareness, self-advocacy skills, and the self-confidence necessary to successfully navigate their way through college and seek out support when needed (National Learning Center for Disabilities, 2017). Once students with disabilities graduate high school and enter institutions of higher education, accommodations will be put in place only if the student self-identifies as having a disability and self-advocates by asking for the appropriate accommodations (Horowitz, Rawe, & Whittaker, 2017).

Success in college is heavily influenced by internal resilience factors such as temperament and self-perception. Low self-esteem and the stigma around disabilities may explain why individuals with learning disabilities enroll in four-year colleges at half the rate of other students. The lack of self-advocacy and self-regulation skills may also explain why students with learning disabilities are less likely to remain in institutes of higher education (Horowitz, Rawe, & Whittaker, 2017).

Although college students bear the burden of self-disclosure, research has found that many students who were identified in high school as having disabilities do not disclose their disabilities when they enter college. Once a student has gained the newfound independence that comes with the college experience, he or she often wants to establish an identity independent of their disability and make a fresh start (National Center for Learning Disabilities, 2017; Young, Michael, & Citro, 2017). Students commonly want to be known for their abilities, not their disabilities.

Some students come from high schools in which disabilities were frowned upon and stigmatized, leaving students with feelings of shame and inadequacy that result from having been labeled as lazy or unintelligent, or as having an unfair advantage over students without disabilities (Horowitz, Rawe, & Whittaker, 2017; National Center for Learning Disabilities, 2017). This fear of continued reprisal often keeps students with disabilities from self-identifying once they reach college.

Society's stigma surrounding disabilities may discourage undergraduates from accessing necessary resources in college. Research has shown that only 24 percent of students with learning disabilities disclosed their disabilities in college (Horowitz, Rawe, & Whittaker, 2017).

Coupled with the fear of being unaccepted socially or academically by their peers, students with disabilities fear receiving a negative response—or worse, no response—from the faculty tasked with providing all students with the knowledge and skills necessary for future success (National Center for Learning Disabilities, 2017). Lack of professional development for college faculty surrounding the nature of disabilities and the legal responsibility to put reasonable accommodations in place contribute to the way students with disabilities are treated if they choose to self-identify.

It is not only the faculty who lack understanding about the accommodation process. Many students do not have a clear understanding of their disabilities and the importance of accommodations in aiding their academic success (National Center for Learning Disabilities, 2017; Young, Michael, & Citro, 2017). Even those students who do recognize the importance of accommodations lack knowledge about what disability services are available, why they are entitled to them, where to find them, and what they need to do to obtain them.

Many students believe that when they enter college they no longer have a disability or need accommodations. According to Horowitz, Rawe, and Whittaker (2017), 69 percent of students with identified learning disabilities in high school did not inform the college of their disability because they no longer considered themselves to have one (Horowitz, Rawe, & Whittiaker, 2017). Only 7 percent of students who still considered themselves as learning disabled did not inform their college. The college years are a key phase of student development, and students generally want to establish their own identities—not only away from their parents but also independent of their disabilities.

Students also may not understand the role accommodations play in their education and future academic success in college and the workplace (Horowitz, Rawe, & Whittaker, 2017). The first step in understanding this is learning what types of disability services are available, where to get them, and what paperwork and documentation is needed for approval of reasonable and appropriate accommodations.

The self-advocacy skills of students with disabilities may be one of the most important factors in determining whether they succeed or fail in college; thus, they need to fully understand their skill deficits prior to their arrival on campus. They should be able to explain their disabilities and the resultant functional limitations as well as their strengths and weaknesses (US Department of Education, 2011).

Students must also accept primary responsibility for their own success or failure in postsecondary education. Students with disabilities entering college are moving from an educational structure in which parents and school administration advocated on their behalf to one in which they are expected to advocate for themselves. Students with disabilities need to understand that while accommodations are guaranteed under federal disability laws, they will not receive accommodations unless they advocate on their own behalf and request them. It is also essential for students to understand that having these accommodations does not guarantee that they will achieve a particular outcome (US Department of Education, 2011).

DIFFERENCES BETWEEN SECONDARY AND POSTSECONDARY SPECIAL EDUCATION SERVICES

Entering college is a time of change for many students, and along with this change comes a change in the laws that protect students with disabilities. Many changes take place during this transition in the way students' disabilities are defined as well as how they are protected and what laws protect them. In a K–12 setting, students are protected under IDEA (IDEA Partnership, n.d.). In order to receive special education services and accommodations under IDEA, a student must qualify by both having a disability and demonstrating a failure to make adequate academic progress.

When a student with a documented disability graduates high school, receives a standard diploma, and moves on to higher education, it is considered a change in placement and terminates the student's eligibility for special education, and the protections under IDEA cease to exist (Horowitz, Rawe, & Whittaker, 2017). The only remaining opportunities available to students to obtain accommodations and supportive services are under the Americans with Disabilities Act (US Department of Labor, n.d., b) and Section 504 of the Rehabilitation Act of 1973 (Young, Michael, & Citro, 2017).

In order to receive services under the Rehabilitation Act, Section 504 requires only that a student have a physical or mental impairment that substantially limits a major life activity and have documentation of such impairment, or be regarded as having such. Major life activities include walking, seeing, hearing, speaking, breathing, learning, working, caring for oneself, and performing manual tasks (US Department of Education, 2011).

As opposed to the requirement under IDEA (IDEA Partnership, n.d.) that secondary schools seek out those students with disabilities, neither Section 504 nor the ADA requires that institutes of higher education actively seek out students with disabilities. Institutions of higher education do not have a duty to identify students with disabilities and are required only to provide accommodations and services. The burden is on the student to notify the appropriate college department of his or her disability and need for academic accommodations (US Department of Education, 2011; Young, Michael, & Citro, 2017).

Once a student with a disability has been identified, the way in which services are provided is different in college than it was in high school. As discussed earlier, in K–12 education IDEA (IDEA Partnership, n.d.) requires that a multidisciplinary team be formed by the school to determine a student's eligibility for services and what services are necessary and beneficial for the student to have. Parents must belong to the team and take an active role in making the essential decisions regarding the type of accommodations the student should receive, which are placed on an IEP (Young, Michael, & Citro, 2017).

At the college level, IEPs no longer exist. A college or university is required to develop a plan for accommodations in collaboration with the student and any other appropriate parties, such as the student's parents or professors. Some colleges still refer to these accommodation plans as 504 plans, while others have done away with that terminology to avoid confusion and instead simply list the necessary accommodations on university letterhead as a formal accommodation approval letter. With the transition to college, family presence and input is no longer required, although it can be requested, and the decisions might be made only by a disability service professional and the student.

ACCOMMODATIONS AT THE COLLEGIATE LEVEL

College Disability Service Departments

Most institutes of higher education accept and admit students with disabilities and provide accommodations such as extended time on tests, classroom note takers, and tutoring to help develop learning strategies or study skills (National Center for Learning Disabilities, 2017). When students enter the postsecondary environment, familiar supports and resources from high school disappear, and it becomes the students' responsibility to make their own educational decisions and advocate on their own behalf (US Department of Education, 2011).

Students have no obligation to inform postsecondary institutions of their disabilities, but students who want academic or other types of accommodations must identify as having a disability (US Department of Education, 2011). Although departmental missions may vary between institutions, disability service providers at the college level seek to create an accessible, inclusive, sustainable learning environment where disabilities are recognized as an aspect of diversity that is integral to the campus community and to society.

Disability service professionals regularly collaborate with all members of an institution's diverse community to ensure that all aspects of campus life—learning, working, and living—are universally accessible for the student with disabilities. Resources, training, and direct services to provide people with disabilities a greater opportunity to achieve their goals are routinely provided (American International College, 2017).

The common goals and objectives of collegiate disability departments are to promote and facilitate access through creative outreach and training, offer collaborative partnerships, provide innovative programs and proactive solutions, support and facilitate students' transition to postsecondary education, have acceptable rates of retention and graduation for students with disabilities, remove campus-wide barriers for people with disabilities, and ensure the effective delivery of appropriate accommodations (American International College, 2017).

Section 504 and the ADA

Institutes of higher education that receive federal funding must be in compliance with the regulations outlined in Section 504 of the Rehabilitation Act as well as Title II of the ADA (US Department of Education, 2016). Section 504 is a civil rights statute designed to prevent discrimination against individuals with disabilities and provides that no otherwise qualified individual with a disability shall be excluded from the participation in any program receiving federal financial assistance solely by virtue of having a disability.

The ADA, which took effect in 1992, was modeled after Section 504. It guarantees equal opportunity for individuals with disabilities in employment, public accommodations, transportation, state and local government services, and telecommunications. The ADA defines an individual with a disability as a person who has a physical or mental impairment that substantially limits a major life activity, has a record or history of such impairment, or is regarded as having such impairment. Under the ADA (US Department of Labor, n.d., b) essential accommodations, such as extended time for tests or technology-based supports, are considered necessary and reasonable for students with documented learning disabilities. Research has shown that students who receive assistance from collegiate disability service departments are more likely to be successful and to complete their education (National Center for Learning Disabilities, 2017).

Documentation

In addition to self-identifying, a student with a disability must provide proof of his or her disability to the appropriate department (Young, Michael, & Citro, 2017). Although parents may provide the disability department with the appropriate and required documentation, this does not promote a student's self-advocacy skills. A student who provides his or her own documentation has the opportunity to sit down with a disability support professional and discuss the nature of the disability, past accommodations, what was helpful and what was not, what accommodations the student would like to have in college, and what available accommodations may be the most appropriate given the nature of the student's disability in a new academic environment.

The trend in disability services is to divide the types of documentation that may be required for accommodation purposes into two categories: primary and secondary documentation. Primary documentation can include a letter prepared by an appropriate professional, such as a medical doctor, psychologist, or other qualified diagnostician, showing that the student has a current disability and a need for reasonable accommodations. The letter should include a diagnosis of the current disability, including the date and how the diagnosis was reached, on appropriate letterhead and signed by the appropriate professional, with their credentials as well as information on how the disability affects a major life activity and academic performance (US Department of Education, 2011; United States Access Board, n.d.).

Secondary types of documentation include a student's narrative or self-report of his or her experience of disability and the barriers and effective and ineffective accommodations he or she has experienced in past schooling. Although IEPs were the backbone of special education services and accommodation in secondary education, they are generally not sufficient by themselves for accommodation purposes as there are differences between postsecondary education and high school education (US Department of Education, 2011).

Disability service professionals should discuss with the student what academic adjustments are appropriate based on the disclosed disability and the student's individual needs. Students with disabilities know themselves the best and possess unique knowledge of their individual disabilities and can speak to the functional challenges they face (US Department of Education, 2011). The impressions and conclusions formed by disability service department professionals during these discussions as well as the observations of the students' language, performance, and strategies may also be used as secondary documentation to support the need for accommodations.

Although the trend in higher education has moved away from diagnostic and medical documentation and is relying more on collaboration with the student and students' self-reporting, the Respond, Innovate, Succeed and Empower (RISE) Act of 2016, recently introduced in the Senate, aims to help students with disabilities succeed in college in two important ways (National Center for Learning Disabilities, 2016). If passed, it will require colleges to accept IEPs or 504 plans as primary evidence of a disability, eliminating the need for students to undergo costly diagnostic testing in order to receive accommodations in college. The RISE Act would also provide $10 million to fund the National Center for College Students with Disabilities (NCCSD), a technical assistance center that would provide information on best practices in helping students with disabilities succeed in postsecondary education (National Center for Learning Disabilities, 2017).

Types of Accommodations

Once a student has applied and been approved for accommodations, it is the student's responsibility to follow through with the accommodation. For example, if the student is approved for extended time on testing, the student does not have to use the time and can instead opt to take the exam in class during the permitted time.

For those students who qualify for services in college, there are many modifications, accommodations, and resources that can be put in place. This is due, in part, to the differences between high school and college and who holds the financial responsibility for putting the resources in place.

Under Section 504, academic accommodations are considered modifications necessary to ensure that academic requirements do not discriminate or have the effect of discriminating on the basis of a disability against an otherwise qualified student (US Department of Education, 2011). Common accommodations that a student might find in both high school and college include extended time for exams, a distraction-free test-taking environment, text-to-speech and/or speech-to-text technology, preferential seating, and note-taking services.

Additional accommodations available at the college level that students are often unaware of include classroom relocation; movement breaks; copies of instructors' notes, PowerPoints, outlines, and study guides; housing and meal plan accommodations; reduced course loads; course substitution; and emotional support animals. Academic adjustments may also include recording devices, sign language interpreters, screen readers, voice recognition, and other adaptive software or hardware for computers and other devices to aid the student's participation in the college's programs and activities.

Public post-secondary institutions are not required to provide personal devices and services such as attendants, individually prescribed devices, or human readers. They are required to give primary consideration to an auxiliary aid or service requested by a student; however, they may opt to provide alternatives if they are effective, especially if the requested aid or service would fundamentally alter the nature of a service, program, or activity or result in undue financial burden to the institution (US Department of Education, 2011).

BARRIERS TO ACCOMMODATIONS IN COLLEGE

The National Center for Learning Disabilities (NCLD) reports that only 17 percent of students with learning disabilities seek accommodations in college (National Center on Learning Disabilities, 2017). One reason for this low number is that many students with learning disabilities view starting college as a fresh start, and they attempt to navigate the experience on their own. Those students who choose to self-identify and disclose their disabilities can have trouble accessing services and supports similar to those they received in high school (National Center for Learning Disabilities, 2017).

One of the most common obstacles to receiving accommodations in college is the lack of information about disability services at the college itself. According to an unpublished 2016 NCLD survey, 45 percent of parents whose children were seeking college accommodations stated that it was difficult to find information about disability services in college (National Center for Learning Disabilities, 2017).

Another obstacle to having the appropriate accommodations put in place in higher education is the documentation requirements. More than half of colleges that require documentation of a disability do not accept IEPs or 504 plans as a primary source of eligible documentation to qualify for accommodations. Due to licensing requirements in such programs as nursing, occupational therapy, teaching, and psychology, some disability service departments may not accept any diagnostic testing that is more than three years old (National Center for Learning Disabilities, 2017).

To make this issue more complicated, there is no set institutional standard regarding documentation of a disability (US Department of Education, 2011). Institutes of higher education are free to set their own requirements, resulting in a great deal of variation in what is considered acceptable documentation. Colleges also widely vary in their disability determinations and are far more restrictive about what types of accommodations are granted to the student, making self-advocacy important (National Center for Learning Disabilities, 2017).

FINAL THOUGHTS

Once the shift from secondary to higher education is made, a student must first self-identify as having a disability then self-disclose this disability to the appropriate department and advocate for the necessary accommodations. Many students do not advocate for themselves in college by disclosing a disability due to the fear of being ostracized socially or academically by their peers and the fear of being unacknowledged or treated differently by faculty and staff.

Students with disabilities may not understand the role accommodations play in their educational careers and, as such, it is imperative that students with disabilities take primary responsibility for their education and seek to disclose their disabilities to the appropriate department on campus and work with the staff to put the appropriate accommodations in place to ensure success.

Disability service providers and departments exist to create accessible, inclusive, and sustainable learning environments where disabilities are recognized as part of diversity within campus communities. Disability service professionals are responsible for collaborating with colleagues across campus to ensure that all aspects of campus life are accessible to students with disabilities.

While colleges are required to put reasonable accommodations in place to level the playing field for students with disabilities, they are not required to provide accommodations that would alter or waive essential academic requirements; alter the nature of a service, program, or activity; or result in undue financial or administrative burden to the college.

It is essential that students with learning disabilities take an active role in their future educational endeavors and investigate potential colleges thoroughly. Postsecondary institutions are free to set their own requirements regarding disability services, resulting in a wide variation in what is considered to be acceptable documentation and appropriate accommodations for students with disabilities (Center for Learning Disabilities, 2017).

POINTS TO REMEMBER

- *Many students believe that when they enter college they no longer have a disability and/or need accommodations. Sixty-nine percent of students with identified learning disabilities in high school did not inform their colleges of their disabilities because they no longer considered themselves to have them (Horowitz, Rawe, & Whittaker, 2017). Students want to be known for their abilities, not their disabilities.*
- *The lack of professional development for college faculty surrounding the nature of disabilities and the legal responsibility to putting reasonable accommodations in place may be contributing factors in students' choice not to disclose their disabilities.*
- *In order to receive accommodations, Section 504 requires that students have a physical or mental impairment that substantially limits a major life activity and have documentation of such impairment. Students with disabilities are guaranteed accommodations under federal disability law, but the achievement of a particular outcome or student success is not guaranteed by the accommodations (US Department of Education, 2011).*

- *To receive accommodations, college students must voluntarily identify themselves as having a disability, identify the accommodations and services they require, disclose this information to the appropriate college department, and provide the required and appropriate documentation (US Department of Education, 2011). Students who receive accommodations are more likely to be successful and complete their education (National Center for Learning Disabilities, 2017).*
- *More than 50 percent of colleges that require documentation of a disability do not accept IEPs or 504 plans as documentation to qualify for accommodations (National Center for Learning Disabilities, 2017). Colleges also may not accept documentation that is too old due to licensing requirements in particular areas of study such as nursing, occupational therapy, teaching, and psychology (National Center for Learning Disabilities, 2017).*

References

Agrawal, J. & Morin, L.L. (2016). Evidence-based practices: Applications of concrete representational abstract framework across math concepts for students with mathematics disabilities. *Learning Disabilities Research & Practice (Wiley-Blackwell)*, *31*(1), 34–44. doi:10. 1111/ldrp.12093

Alquarini, T. & Gut, D. (2012). Critical components of successful inclusion of students with severe disabilities: Literature review. *International Journal of Special Education*, *27*, 1–18. Retrieved from https://eric.ed.gov/?id=EJ979712

Alvarez, B. (2016). Promising changes for special education under ESSA. *NeaToday*. Retrieved from http://neatoday.org/2016/06/30/special-education-essa

American Federation of Teachers. (n.d.). *Every Student Succeeds Act: A new day in public education*. Retrieved from https://www.aft.org/sites/default/files/essa_faq.pdf

American Federation of Teachers. (2012). *Creating a classroom team: How teachers and paraprofessionals can make working together work*. Retrieved from http://www.ctteam.org/wp-content/uploads/2012/05/classroom_team.pdf

American International College. (2017). *Center for Disability Services and Academic Accommodations*. Retrieved from https://my.aic.edu/ICS/Campus_Life/Center_for_Disability_Services/

American Occupational Therapy Association. (2015). *Even after 40 years, new ideas for IDEA*. Retrieved from https://www.aota.org/publications-news/aotanews/2015/individuals-disabilities-education-act.aspx

American Psychiatric Association. (2016). *What is specific learning disorder?* Retrieved from https://www.psychiatry.org/patients-families/specific-learning-disorder/what-is-specific-learning-disorder

American Speech-Language-Hearing Association (ASHA). (2014a). *Attention deficit/hyperactivity disorder*. Retrieved from http://www.asha.org/public/speech/disorders/ADHD/

American Speech-Language-Hearing Association (ASHA). (2014b). *Understanding the differences between auditory processing, speech and language disorders, and reading disorders*. Retrieved from http://www.asha.org/uploadedFiles/Resource-for-DoJ-10-2014.pdf

Archer, A. & Hughes, C. (2011). *Explicit instruction: Effective and efficient teaching*. New York, NY: Guilford Press.

Armendariz, G. & Jung, A. (2016). Response to intervention vs. severe discrepancy model: Identification of students with specific learning disabilities. *Journal of Special Education*. *5*(1). Retrieved from http://files.eric.ed.gov/fulltext/EJ1127748.pdf

Ashraf, F. & Najam, N. (2015). Comorbidity of anxiety disorder and major depression among girls with learning disabilities. *Pakistan Journal of Medical Research*, *54*(4). Retrieved from https://www.researchgate.net/publication/304626930

Atiles, J., Jones, J., & Kim, H. (2012). Field experience + inclusive ECE classrooms = increased preservice teacher efficacy in working with students with developmental delays or disabilities. *Educational Research Quarterly, 36*(2), 62–85.

Beauchemin, J., Hutchins, T., & Patterson, F. (2008). Mindfulness meditation may lessen anxiety, promote social skills, and improve academic performance among adolescents with learning disabilities. *Complementary Health Practice Review, 13*(1), 35–45. doi:10.1177/1533210107311624

Bellis, T.J. (2017). *Understanding auditory processing disorders in children.* Retrieved from http://www.asha.org/public/hearing/Understanding-Auditory-Processing-Disorders-in-Children/

Bett, H.K. (2016). The cascade model of teachers' continuing professional development in Kenya: A time for change? *Cogent Education, 3*(1). Retrieved from https://eric.ed.gov/?id=EJ1138551

Biggs, E.E., Gilson, C.B., & Carter, E.E. (2016). Accomplishing more together: Influences to the quality of professional relationships between special educators and paraprofessionals. *Research and Practice for Persons with Severe Disabilities, 41*(4) 256–272. doi:10.1177/1540796916665604

Bjorn, P., Aro, M., Koponen, T., Fuchs, L., & Fuchs, D. (2016). The many faces of special education within the RTI frameworks in the United States and Finland. *Learning Disabilities Quarterly, 39*(1), 58–66. doi:10.1177/0731948715594787

Blake, J., Lund, E., Zhou, Q., Kwok, O., & Benz, M. (2012). National prevalence rates of bully victimization among students with disabilities in the United States. *School Psychology Quarterly, 27*, 210–222. doi:10.1037/spq0000008

Blatchford, P., Webster, R., & Russell, A. (2012). *Reassessing the impact of teaching assistants: How research challenges practice and policy.* Abingdon, Oxon: Routledge.

Bowe, J. & Gore, J. (2017). Reassembling teacher professional development: the case for quality teaching rounds. *Teachers and Teaching: Theory & Practice.* doi:10.1080/13540602.2016.1206522

Bright Hub Education. (2016). *Is ADHD considered a learning disability?* Retrieved from http://www.brighthubeducation.com/special-ed-behavioral-disorders/62948-learn-why-adhd-is-not-considered-a-learning-disability/

British Columbia Ministry of Education and British Columbia School Superintendent's Association (2011). *Supporting students with learning disabilities: A guide for teachers.* Victoria, BC: Province of British Columbia. Retrieved from http://www.bced.gov.bc.ca/specialed/docs/learning_disabilities_guide.pdf

British Columbia Teachers Federation. (2017). *Professional development and support.* Retrieved from https://bctf.ca/ProfessionalDevelopment.aspx

Brock, M.E. (2015). Effects of a professional development package to prepare special education paraprofessionals to implement evidence-based practice. *Journal of Special Education, 49*(1), 39–51. doi:10.1177/0022466913501882

Browder D., Wood L., Thompson J., & Ribuffo C. (2014). *Evidence-based practices for students with severe disabilities.* Gainesville, FL: CEEDAR Center. Retrieved from http://ceedar.education.ufl.edu/wp-content/uploads/2014/09/IC-3_FINAL_03-03-15.pdf

Bryant, B., Ok, M., Kang, E., Kim, M., Lang, R., Bryant, D., & Pfannestiel, K. (2015). Performance of fourth grade students with learning disabilities on multiplication facts comparing teacher mediated and technology mediated interventions: A preliminary investigation. *Journal of Behavior Education, 24*, 255–272. doi:10.1007/s10864-015-9218-z

Bryant, D. & Bryant, B. (2011). *Assistive technology for people with disabilities* (2nd ed.). Boston, MA: Allyn & Bacon.

Burns, M. (2011). *Distance education for teacher training: modes, models, and methods.* Washington, DC: Education Development Center. Retrieved from http://idd.edc.org/sites/idd.edc.org/files/Distance Education for Teacher Training by Mary Burns EDC.pdf

Burns, M. (2014). *Five models of teacher-centered professional development.* Retrieved from http://www.globalpartnership.org/blog/five-models-teacher-centered-professional-development

CAST. (2017a). *About CAST.* Retrieved from http://www.cast.org/about#.Waq82IpJnow

CAST. (2017b). Free learning tools. Retrieved from http://www.cast.org/our-work/learning-tools.html#.WarAOIpJnow

Center for Appropriate Dispute Resolution in Special Education. (2014). *IDEA special education resolution meetings: A guide for parents and youth (ages 3–21)*. Retrieved from http://www.cadreworks.org/sites/default/files/resources/ResolutionMeetingParentGuide_FINAL_10.24.14.pdf

Center for Parent Information and Resources. (2017). *State complaint, in detail*. Retrieved from http://www.parentcenterhub.org/details-statecomplaint/

Centers for Disease Control and Prevention. (2017). *Attention-deficit/hyperactivity disorder (ADHD)*. Retrieved from https://www.cdc.gov/ncbddd/adhd/data.html

Chiang, H., Walsh, E., Shanahan, T., Gentile, C., Maccarone, A., Waits, T., Carlson, B., & Rikoon, S. (2017). *An exploration of instructional practices that foster language development and comprehension: Evidence from prekindergarten through grade 3 in Title I schools (NCEE 2017-4024)*. Washington, DC: National Center for Education Evaluation and Regional Assistance, Institute of Education Sciences, US Department of Education. Retrieved from https://ies.ed.gov/ncee/pubs/20174024/pdf/20174024.pdf

Ciullo, S., Falcomata, T.S., Pfannenstiel, K., & Billingsley, G. (2015). Improving learning with science and social studies text using computer-based concept maps for students with disabilities. *Behavior Modification, 39*(1), 117–135. doi:10.1177/0145445514552890

Coalition for Community Schools, Institute for Educational Leadership & National Association of School Psychologists. (2016). *Nine elements of effective school community partnerships to address student mental health, physical health, and overall wellness*. Retrieved from http://www.nasponline.org/assets/documents/Research and Policy/Advocacy Resources/Community Schools White Paper_Jan_2016.pdf

Collaborative for Academic, Social and Emotional Learning. (2017). *What is SEL?* Retrieved from http://www.casel.org/what-is-sel/

Committee for Children. (2013). *The second step program and the bully prevention unit: A powerful combination*. Retrieved from http://www.cfchildren.org/blog/2013/05/the-second-step-program-and-the-bullying-prevention-unit-a-powerful-combination/

Committee for Children. (2017). *Finding lifelong success with social-emotional learning*. Retrieved from http://www.cfchildren.org/programs/social-emotional-learning/

Connecticut State Department of Education (2012). *Guidelines for training and support of paraprofessionals: Working with students birth to 21*. Retrieved from http://www.sde.ct.gov/sde/lib/sde/pdf/cali/guidelines_paraprofessionals.pdf

Connelly, V. & Dockrell, J. (2016). Writing development and instruction for students with learning disabilities. In MacAuthur, C., Graham, S., & Fitzgerald, J. (Eds.), *Handbook of writing research* (pp. 211–226). New York, NY. Guilford Press.

Consortium for Citizens with Learning Disabilities. (2015). *IDEA at 40: Celebrating progress in educating students with disabilities*. Retrieved from http://www.council-for-learning-disabilities.org/wp-content/uploads/2015/11/IDEAat40-Nov2015.pdf

Cook, B.G. & Odom, S.L. (2013). *Evidence-based practices and implementation science in special education*. Retrieved from https://eric.ed.gov/?id=EJ1013632

Cornell Law School. (n.d. a). *Child's status during proceedings. 34 CFR §300.518*. Retrieved from https://www.law.cornell.edu/cfr/text/34/300.518

Cornell Law School. (n.d. b) *Consent. 34 CFR §300.9*. Retrieved from https://www.law.cornell.edu/cfr/text/34/300.9

Cornell Law School. (n.d. c). *Due process complaint. 34 CFR §300.508*. Retrieved from https://www.law.cornell.edu/cfr/text/34/300.508

Cornell Law School. (n.d. d). *Filing a complaint. 34 CFR 300.153*. Retrieved from https://www.law.cornell.edu/cfr/text/34/300.153

Cornell Law School. (n.d. e). *Hearing rights. 34 CFR §300.512*. Retrieved from https://www.law.cornell.edu/cfr/text/34/300.512

Cornell Law School. (n.d. f). *Independent educational evaluations. 34 CFR §300.502*. Retrieved from https://www.law.cornell.edu/cfr/text/34/300.502

Cornell Law School. (n.d. g). *Mediation. 34 CFR §300.506*. Retrieved from https://www.law.cornell.edu/cfr/text/34/300.506

Cornell Law School. (n.d. h). *Notice to parents.* 34 CFR §300.612. Retrieved from https://www.law.cornell.edu/cfr/text/34/300.612

Cornell Law School. (n.d. i). *Prior notice by the public agency; content of notice.* 34 CFR §300.503. Retrieved from https://www.law.cornell.edu/cfr/text/34/300.503

Cornell Law School. (n.d. j). *Safeguards.* 34 CFR §300.623. Retrieved from https://www.law.cornell.edu/cfr/text/34/300.623

Cornell Law School. (n.d. k). *Amendment of records at parents request.* 34 CFR §300.618. Retrieved from https://www.law.cornell.edu/cfr/text/34/300.618

Council for Exceptional Children (CEC). (1997). *CEC policy manual* (sec. 3, pp. 71–92). Retrieved from https://www.cec.sped.org/Policy-and-Advocacy/CEC-Professional-Policies/Special-Education-in-the-Schools

Council for Exceptional Children (CEC). (2014). *CEC standards for evidence based practices in special education.* Arlington, VA: Council for Exceptional Children. Retrieved from https://www.cec.sped.org/~/media/Files/Standards/Evidence based Practices and Practice/EBP FINAL.pdf

Council for Exceptional Children (CEC). (2017). *Engaging the potential.* Retrieved from https://www.cec.sped.org/Professional-Development

Council of Chief State School Officers. (2017). *ESSA: key provisions and implications for students with disabilities.* Retrieved from http://www.oregon.gov/ode/rules-and-policies/ESSA/ESSAResources/Documents/ESSA_Key_Provisions_Implications_for_SWD.pdf

Dahle, A., Knivsberg, A., & Andressen, A. (2011). Coexisting problem behaviour in severe dyslexia. *Journal of Research in Special Educational Needs, 11,* 162–170. doi:10.1111/j.1471-3802.2010.01190

Darling-Hammond, L., Hyler, M.E., & Gardner, M. (2017). *Effective teacher professional development.* Palo Alto, CA: Learning Policy Institute. Retrieved from https://learningpolicyinstitute.org/sites/default/files/product-files/Effective_Teacher_Professional_Development_REPORT.pdf

Demonte, J. (2013). *High-quality professional development for teachers: Supporting teacher training to improve student learning.* Washington, DC: Center for American Progress. Retrieved from https://www.americanprogress.org/wp-content/uploads/2013/07/DeMonteLearning4Teachers-1.pdf

Department of Defense Educational Activity. (2007). *Guidelines for student support teams (SST).* Retrieved from http://www.dodea.edu/Curriculum/specialEduc/upload/DoDEA_SST.pdf

Desimone, L.M. & Pak, K. (2017). Instructional coaching as high-quality professional development. *Theory into Practice, 56*(1). doi:10.1080/00405841.2016.1241947

Diaz-Maggioli, G. (2017). *Teacher-centered professional development.* Retrieved from http://www.ascd.org/publications/books/104021.aspx

Disabilities, Opportunities, Internetworking, and Technology. (2017a). *Statistics.* Retrieved from http://www.washington.edu/doit/statistics

Disabilities, Opportunities, Internetworking, and Technology. (2017b). *What is the Individuals with Disabilities Act?* Retrieved from http://www.washington.edu/doit/what-individuals-disabilities-education-act

Douglas, S.N., Chapin, S.E., & Nolan, J.F. (2016). Special education teachers' experiences supporting and supervising paraeducators: Implications for special and general education settings. *Teacher Education and Special Education, 39*(1), 60–74. doi:10.1177/0888406415616443

Durlak, J., Dymnicki, A., Taylor, R., Weissberg, R., & Schellinger, K. (2011). The impact of enhancing students' social and emotional learning: a meta-analysis of school based universal interventions. *Child Development, 82,* 405–432. Retrieved from https://www.ncbi.nlm.nih.gov/pubmed/21291449

Dyscalculia.org. (2017). *What is Dyscalculia?* Retrieved from http://www.dyscalculia.org/dyscalculia

Early Childhood Technical Assistance Center (ECTA Center). (2017). *Family rights, privacy, procedural safeguards and complaint resolution under IDEA.* Retrieved from http://ectacenter.org/topics/procsafe/procsafe.asp

Ellis, E.S., Worthington, L., & Larkin, M.J. (1994). *Research synthesis on effective teaching.* Retrieved from https://pdfs.semanticscholar.org/d8a5/024b1e724597c8f3612ebc 008522050112e5.pdf

Espelage, D., Rose, C., & Polanin, J. (2016). Social emotional learning program to promote prosocial and academic skills among middle school students with disabilities. *Remedial and Special Education, 37*(6), 323–332. doi:10.1177/0741932515627475

eTools4Education. (2017). *Learner-centered professional development.* Retrieved from http://www.online-distance-learning-education.com/learner-centered.html

Ficarra, L. & Quinn, K. (2014). Teachers' facility with evidence-based classroom management practices: An investigation of teacher preparation programs and in-service conditions. *Journal of Teacher Education for Sustainability, 16*(2), 71–87. Retrieved from http://files.eric.ed.gov/fulltext/EJ1108117.pdf

Flanagan, S. & Bouck, E. (2015). Mapping out the details: Supporting struggling writers' written expression with concept mapping. *Preventing School Failure, 59*(4), 244–252. Retrieved from https://eric.ed.gov/?id=EJ1069831

Flores, M., Hinton, V., Strozier, S., & Terry, S. (2014). Using the concrete-representational-abstract sequence and the strategic instruction model to teach computation to teach students with autism spectrum disorders and developmental disabilities. *Education and Training in Autism and Developmental Disabilities, 49*(4), 547–554. Retrieved from http://daddcec.org/Portals/0/ETADD49(4)_547-554.pdf

Ford, J. (2013). Educating students with learning disabilities. *Electronic Journal for Inclusive Education, 3*(1). Retrieved from http://corescholar.libraries.wright.edu/cgi/viewcontent.cgi?article=1154&context=ejie

French, N.K. (n.d.). *Working effectively with paraeducators.* Retrieved from http://www.specialconnections.ku.edu/?q=collaboration/working_effectively_with_paraeducators

Fuchs, D., Fuchs, L., & Compton, D. (2012). Smart RTI: A next-generation approach to multilevel prevention. *Exceptional Children, 78,* 263–279. doi:10.1177/0014402 91207800301

Fulton, L. Nguyen, M., Watkins, E., & Vaughn, C. (2012). The cascade model of professional development. Retrieved from https://prezi.com/sqxrxhc9liry/cascade-model/

Generation Ready. (2013). *Raising student achievement through professional development.* Retrieved from http://www.generationready.com/wp-content/uploads/2013/10/PD-White-Paper.pdf

Goe, L. & Matlach, L. (2014). *Supercharging student success: Policy levers for helping paraprofessionals have a positive influence in the classroom.* Retrieved from https://eric.ed.gov/?id=ED558020

Grant, K.B. & Ray, J.A. (2016). *Home, school, and community collaboration: Culturally responsive family engagement* (3rd ed.). Thousand Oaks, CA: SAGE.

Graves, J.C. & Graves, C. (2016). *Writing effective IEP goals.* Retrieved from http://fcsn.org/rtsc/wp-content/uploads/sites/2/2016/11/Writing-IEP-Goals-pdf.pdf

Green, T.R. & Allen, M.E. (2015). Professional development urban schools: What do the teachers say? *Journal of Inquiry and Action in Education, 6*(2), 53–79. Retrieved from https://eric.ed.gov/?id=EJ1133585

Gueldner, B. & Feuerborn, L. (2016). Integrating mindfulness-based practices into social and emotional learning: a case application. *Mindfulness, 7,* 164–175. doi:10.1007/s12671-015-0423-6

Hall, C. (2016). Inference instruction for struggling readers: a synthesis of intervention research. *Educational Psychology Review, 28*(1), 1–22. doi:10.1007/s10648-014-9295-x

Hanover Research. (2013). *Professional development for personalized learning practices.* Arlington, VA: Hanover Research. Retrieved from http://www.hanoverresearch.com/media/Professional-Development-for-Personalized-Learning-Practices.pdf

Harn, B., Parisi, D., & Stoolmiller, M. (2013). Balancing fidelity with flexibility and fit: What do we really know about fidelity of implementation in schools? *Exceptional Children, 79*(2), 181–193. doi:10.1177/001440291307900204

Harris, K. & Graham, S. (2013). An adjective is a word hanging down from a noun: Learning to write and students with learning disabilities. *Annals of Dyslexia, 63*(1), 65–79. doi:10.1007/s11881-011-0057-x

Harris, K. R., Graham, S., Aitken, A. A., Barkel, J., Houston, J., & Ray, A. (2017). Teaching spelling, writing, and reading for writing: Powerful evidence-based practices. *Teaching Exceptional Children, 49*(4), 262–272. doi:10.1177/0040059917697250

Heitin, R. (n.d.). Writing IEP goals. Retrieved from http://www.ldonline.org/article/42058

Hoover, J. & Sarris, J. (2014). Six essential instructional roles to implement response to intervention models: Perceptions of highly qualified special educators. *American Journal of Educational Research, 2*(5), 257–266. doi:10.12691/education-2-5-4

Hoppey, D. (2013). Linking action research to response to intervention (RtI): The strategy implementation project. *Networks: An Online Journal for Teacher Research, 15*(1), 1–10. Retrieved from http://journals.sfu.ca/uwmadison/index.php/networks/article/view/624/625

Horowitz, S. H., Rawe, J., & Whittaker, M.C. (2017). The state of learning disabilities: Understanding the 1 in 5. New York, NY: National Center for Learning Disabilities. Retrieved from   https://www.ncld.org/wp-content/uploads/2017/03/Executive-Summary.Fin_.03142017.pdf

Hurlbut, A. & Tunks, J. (2016). Elementary preservice teachers' experiences with response to intervention. *Teacher Education Quarterly, 43*(3), 25–48. Retrieved from http://files.eric.ed.gov/fulltext/EJ1110288.pdf

IDEA Partnership. (2004). *About IDEA.* Retrieved from: https://sites.ed.gov/idea/about-idea/

IDEA Partnership. (n.d.). *Individuals with Disabilities Education Improvement Act.* 34 CFR§612.8(c)(10), 2004. Retrieved from http://www.ideapartnership.org/topics-database/idea-2004.html

Inner Resilience Program. (2016). *Core programs.* Retrieved from http://www.innerresilience-tidescenter.org/programs.html

Inspiration Software. (2017). *Teaching and learning with graphic organizers.* Retrieved from http://www.inspiration.com/visual-learning/graphic-organizers

Institute of Education Sciences. (n.d.). *What works clearinghouse.* Retrieved from https://ies.ed.gov/ncee/wwc/

International Dyslexia Association. (2017a). *Dyslexia basics.* Retrieved from https://dyslexiaida.org/dyslexia-basics/

International Dyslexia Association. (2017b). *Understanding dysgraphia.* Retrieved from https://dyslexiaida.org/understanding-dysgraphia/

Jericho School District. (2017). *The pros and cons of individual paraprofessionals or teacher aides.* Retrieved from http://web.jerichoschools.org/jackson/teachers/conger/Pros%20and%20Cons%20of%20Individual%20Teacher%20Aides.pdf

Kaldenberg, E., Watt, S., & Therrien, W. (2014). Reading instruction in science for students with learning disabilities: a meta-analysis. *Learning Disabilities Quarterly, 38*(3), 160–173. doi:10.1177/0731948714550204

Kamenetz, A. (2016). School testing 2016: Same tests, different stakes. NPR *Morning Edition.* Retrieved from http://www.npr.org/sections/ed/2015/12/28/459068910/school-testing-2016-same-tests-different-stakes

Kang, E.Y., McKenna, J., Arden, S., & Ciullo, S. (2015). Integrated reading and writing interventions for students with learning disabilities: A review of the literature. *Learning Disabilities Research & Practice, 31*(1), 22–33. doi:10.1111/ldrp.12091

Kim, W., Linan-Thompson, S., & Misquitta, R. (2012). Critical factors in reading comprehension instruction for students with LD: A research synthesis. *Learning Disabilities Research & Practice, 27*(2), 66–78. doi:10.1111/j.1540-5826.2012.00352.x

King Thorius, K., and Maxcy, B. (2015). Critical practice analysis of special education policy: An RTI example. *Remedial and Special Education, 36*(2), 116–124. doi:10.1177/0741932514550812

King Thorius, K., Maxcy, B., Macey, E., & Cox, A. (2014). A critical practice analysis of response to intervention appropriation in an urban school. *Remedial and Special Education, 35*(5), 287–299. doi:10.1177/0741932514522100

King Thorius, K. & Sullivan, A.L. (2013). Interrogating instruction and intervention in RTI research with students identified as English language learners. *Reading & Writing Quarterly: Overcoming Learning Difficulties, 29*(1). doi:10.1080/10573569.2013.741953

Klein, A. (2015). No child left behind: An overview. *Ed Week.* Retrieved from http://www.edweek.org/ew/section/multimedia/no-child-left-behind-overview-definition-summary.html

Kratochwill, T.R., Hitchcock, J., Horner, R.H., Levin, J.R., Odom, S.L., Rindskopf, D., & Shadish, W.R.M. (2013). Single-case intervention research design standards. *Remedial and Special Edication, 34*(1), 26–38. doi:10.1177/0741932512452794

Kretlow, A. & Helf, S. (2013). Teacher implementation of evidence-based practices in tier 1: A national survey. *Teacher Education and Special Education, 36*(3), 167–185. doi:10.1177/0888406413489838

Kuo, N. (2015). Understanding the philosophical foundations of disabilities to maximize the potential of response to intervention. *Edcuational Philosophy and Theory, 47*(7), 647–660. doi:10.1080/00131857.2014.905763

Learning Disabilities Association of America (LDA). (2017). *Types of learning disabilities.* Retrieved from https://ldaamerica.org/types-of-learning-disabilities/

Learning Forward: The Professional Learning Association. (2015). *Learning opportunities.* Retrieved from https://learningforward.org/learning-opportunities

Ledford, J.R., Zimmerman, K.N., Harbin, E.R., & Ward, S.E. (2017). Improving use of evidence-based instructional practices for paraprofessionals. *Focus on Autism and Other Developmental Disabilities.* Prepublished April 8, 2017. doi:10.1177/1088357617699178

Legal Framework. (2015). *Procedures for amending education records.* Retrieved from https://framework.esc18.net/display/Webforms/ESC18-FW-Summary.aspx?FID=193

Leonard, J.A. (2012). Changing roles: Special education teachers in a response to intervention model. *Honors Scholar Theses,* 246. Retrieved from http://digitalcommons.uconn.edu/srhonors_theses/246/

Library of Congress. (n.d.). *About the program: Teaching with primary sources.* Retrieved from http://www.loc.gov/teachers/tps/about/

Library of Congress. (2017). *Professional development.* Retrieved from http://www.loc.gov/teachers/professionaldevelopment/

Litvinov, A. (2017). *Bipartisan bill urges full funding for special ed. in face of Trump-DeVos cuts to IDEA.* Retrieved from http://educationvotes.nea.org/2017/06/16/bipartisan-bill-urges-full-funding-special-ed-face-trump-devos-cuts-idea/

Maheady, L., Rafferty, L., Patti, A., and Budin, S. (2016). Leveraging change: Influencing the implemtation of evidence-based practice to improve outcomes for students with disabilities. *Learning Dsiabilities: A Contemporary Journal, 14*(2), 109–120. Retrieved from http://www.ldw-ldcj.org/index.php/open-access-articles/8-testblog/61-leveraging-evidence-based-practices-from-policy-to-action.html

Malow, M. (2015). Social-emotional development—Learning disabilities and anxiety: Common undesirable partners. *Learning Disabilities Worldwide, 8*(2). Retrieved from https://www.ldworldwide.org/single-post/2015/01/01/V8-2-Social-Emotional-Development---Learning-Disabilities-and-Anxiety-Common-Undesirable-Partners

Mammarella, I., Ghisi, M., Bomba, M., Bottesi, G., Caviola, S., Broggi, F., & Nacinovich, R. (2016). Anxiety and depression in children with nonverbal learning disabilities, reading disabilities, or typical development. *Journal of Learning Disabilities, 49*(2), 130–139. doi:10.1177/0022219414529336

Marzano, R.J., Pickering, D.J., & Pollock, J.E. (2001). *Classroom instruction that works: Research-based strategies for increasing student achievement.* Alexandria, VA: ASCD. Retrieved from https://eric.ed.gov/?id=ED450096

Mason-Williams, L., Frederick, J.R., & Mulchay, C.A. (2015). Building adaptive expertise and practice-based evidence: Applying the implementation stages framework to special eduation teacher preparation. *Teacher Education and Special Education, 38*(3), 207–220. doi:10.1177/0888406414551285

Massachusetts Advisory Councils to the Board of Elementary and Secondary Education. (2017). *Annual reports for 2014–2015: Special Education State Advisory Council annual report.* Retrieved from http://www.doe.mass.edu/bese/councils/

Massachusetts Department of Education. (2013). *Parent's notice of procedural safeguards.* Retrieved from http://www.doe.mass.edu/sped/prb/pnps.pdf

Massachusetts Department of Elementary and Secondary Education. (n.d.). *MTSS quick reference guide: Student support teams (SSTs).* Retrieved from http://www.doe.mass.edu/sfss/student-support-teams.pdf

Massachusetts Department of Elementary and Secondary Education. (2017). *The special education advisory council.* Retrieved from http://www.doe.mass.edu/bese/councils/sped/

Massachusetts Executive Office for Administration and Finance. (2017). *Mediation.* Retrieved from http://www.mass.gov/anf/hearings-and-appeals/bureau-of-special-education-appeals-bsea/mediation/

Masters in Special Education Program Guide. (2017a). *5 most common learning disabilities.* Retrieved from http://www.masters-in-special-education.com/lists/5-most-common-learning-disabilities/

Masters in Special Education Program Guide. (2017b). *What is a paraprofessional in special education?* Retrieved from http://www.masters-in-special-education.com/faq/paraprofessional-special-education/

McGovern, J., Lowe, P., & Hill, J. (2016). Relationships between trait anxiety, demographic variables, and school adjustment in students with specific learning disabilities. *Journal of Child and Family Studies, 25*(6), 1724–1734. doi:10.1007/s10826-015-0348-7

McHatton, P. & Parker, A. (2013). Purposeful preparation: Longitudinally exploring inclusion attitudes of general and special education pre-service teachers. *Teacher Education and Special Education, 36*(3), 186–203. doi:10.1177/0888406413491611

Meiklejohn, J., Phillips, C., Freedman, M., Griffin, M., Biegel, G., Roach, A., & Saltzman, A. (2012). Integrating mindfulness training into K12 education: fostering the resilience of teachers and students. *Mindfulness, 3*(4), 291–307. Retrieved from http://www.mindful-well-being.com/wp-content/uploads/2014/07/Meiklejohn-et-al-2012.pdf

Meyer, A., Rose, D., & Gordon, D. (2014). *Universal design for learning: theory and practice.* Wakefield, MA: CAST.

Milligan, K., Badali, P., & Spiroiu, F. (2015). Using Integra Mindfulness Martial Arts to address self-regulation challenges in youth with learning disabilities: A qualitative exploration. *Journal of Child and Family Studies, 24*, 562–575. doi:10.1007/s10826-013-9868-1

Mitchell, B., Deshler, D., & Lenz, B.K. (2012). Examining the role of the special educator in a response to intervention model. *Learning Disabilities : A Contemporary Journal, 10*(2), 53–74. Retrieved from https://eric.ed.gov/?id=EJ998225

Miyata, C. (2016). *OTF supports teachers' self-directed professional development.* Retrieved from https://literacyteaching.net/tag/self-directed-professional-development/

Mugurussa, T. (2013). *The student success team process: Tips for making it successful.* Retrieved from https://www.scholastic.com/teachers/blog-posts/tiffani-mugurussa/student-success-team-process-tips-making-it-successful/

The Nation's Report Card. (2015). *Mathematics.* Retrieved from https://www.nationsreportcard.gov/reading_math_2015/#?grade=4

National Activities to Improve Education of Children with Disabilities. (2004). *Subchapter IV—National activities to improve education of children with disabilities.* Retrieved from http://corpuslegalis.com/us/code/title20/national-activities-to-improve-education-of-children-with-disabilities

National Archives. (2017). *Professional development.* Retrieved from https://www.archives.gov/education/professional-development

National Association of Special Education Teachers (NASET). (n.d.). *NASET LD report #3: Characteristics of children with learning disabilities.* Retrieved from https://www.naset.org/fileadmin/user_upload/LD_Report/Issue__3_LD_Report_Characteristic_of_LD.pdf

National Center for Education Statistics (NCES). (2012). *The nation's report card: Writing 2011 (NECES 2012-470).* Washington, DC: Institute of Education Sciences, US Department of Education. Retrieved from https://nces.ed.gov/nationsreportcard/pdf/main2011/2012470.pdf

National Center for Education Statistics (NCES). (2016a). *The condition of education 2016.* Washington, DC: Institute of Education Sciences, US Department of Education. Retrieved from https://nces.ed.gov/pubsearch/pubsinfo.asp?pubid=2016144

National Center for Education Statistics (NCES). (2016b). Fast facts. Retrieved from https://nces.ed.gov/fastfacts/display.asp?id=372

National Center for Education Statistics (NCES). (2017a). Children and youth with disabilities. In *The condition of education 2017.* Washington, DC: Institute of Education Sciences, US Department of Education. Retrieved from https://nces.ed.gov/programs/coe/indicator_cgg.asp

National Center for Education Statistics (NCES). (2017b) Disability rates and employment status by educational attainment. In *The condition of education 2017.* Washington, DC: Institute of Educational Sciences, US Department of Education. Retrieved from https://nces.ed.gov/programs/coe/indicator_tad.asp

National Center for Learning Disabilities (2014). *The state of learning disabilities* (3rd ed.). New York, NY: NCLD. Retrieved from http://www.ncld.org/wp-content/uploads/2014/11/2014-State-of-LD.pdf

National Center for Learning Disabilities. (2016). *The RISE Act: Making college accessible for students with disabilities.* Retrieved from https://www.ncld.org/wp-content/uploads/2016/12/RISE-ACT-One-SheeterD6.pdf

National Center for Learning Disabilities. (2017). *The state of LD: Transitioning to life after high school.* Retrieved from https://www.ncld.org/transitioning-to-life-after-high-school

National Center for Technology Innovation. (2008). *Finding alternative sources of funding for assistive technology.* Retrieved from http://www.ldonline.org/article/6239/?theme=print

National Center on Universal Design for Learning. (2017). *Universal Design for Learning guidelines.* Retrieved from http://www.udlcenter.org/aboutudl/udlguidelines_theorypractice

National Education Association. (2015). *Getting educated: Paraeducators.* Retrieved from http://www.nea.org/home/18605.htm

National Education Association. (2017). *Professional development.* Retrieved from http://www.nea.org/home/30998.htm

National PTA. (n.d.). *Report: The positive relationship between family involvement and student success.* Retrieved from https://www.pta.org/programs/content.cfm?ItemNumber=1459

National Reading Panel. (2001). *Teaching children to read: An evidence-based assessment of the scientific research literature on reading and its implications for reading instruction.* Rockville, MD: National Institute of Child Health and Human Development, National Institutes of Health. Retrieved from https://www.nichd.nih.gov/publications/pubs/nrp/Documents/report.pdf

National Research Council. (2012). *Education for life and work: Developing transferable knowledge and skills in the 21st century.* Washington, DC: National Academies Press. doi:10.17226/13398

Neal, A. (2013). *Training pre-service teachers in response to intervention: A survey of teacher candidates* (Unpublished doctoral dissertation). Brigham Young University, Provo, UT. Retrieved from http://scholarsarchive.byu.edu/cgi/viewcontent.cgi?article=4701&context=etd

Nelson, J. & Harwood, H. (2011). Learning disabilities and anxiety: A meta-analysis. *Journal of Learning Disabilities, 44*(1), 3–17. doi:10.1177/0022219409359939

Obiakor, F., Harris, M., Mutua, K., Rotatori, A., & Algozzine, B. (2012). Making inclusion work in general education classrooms. *Education and Treatment of Children, 35*(3), 477–490. Retrieved from https://eric.ed.gov/?id=EJ999342

Ok, M., Kim, M., Kang, E., & Bryant, B. (2016). How to find good apps: An evaluation rubric for instructional apps for teaching students with learning disabilities. *Intervention in School and Clinic, 51*(4), 244–252. doi:10.1177/1053451215589179

Open Circle Getting to the Heart of Learning. *Welcome.* Retrieved from https://www.open-circle.org/

Pacer Center. (2017). *Know your parental rights: The meaning and importance of prior written notice and parent consent.* Retrieved from http://www.pacer.org/parent/php/php-c232.pdf

Psychology Today. (2017). Learning disability. Retrieved from https://www.psychologytoday. com/conditions/learning-disability

Rethink. (2017). *Why self-directed professional development matters for educators.* Retrieved from   http://rethinkrethink.com/blog/2017/03/13/why-self-directed-professional-development -matters-for-educators/

Sansosti, F., Goss, S., & Noltemeyer, A. (2011). Perspectives of special education directors on response to intervention in secondary schools. *Contemporary School Psychology, 15,* 9–20. Retrieved from http://files.eric.ed.gov/fulltext/EJ934702.pdf

Satsangi, R. & Bouck, E. (2014). Using virtual manipulative instruction to teach the concepts of area and perimeter to secondary students with disabilities. *Learning Disabilities Quarterly, 38*(3), 174–186. doi:10.1177/0731948714550101

Scheeler, M., Budin, S., & Markelz, A. (2016). The role of teacher preparation in evidence-based practices in schools. *Learning Disabilities: A Contemporary Journal, 14*(2), 171–187. Retrieved from http://www.ldw-ldcj.org/index.php/open-access-articles/8-testblog/64-the-role-of-teacher-preparation-in-promoting-evidence-based-practice-in-schools.html

Scruggs, T., Mastropieri, M., & Marshak, L. (2012). Peer-mediated instruction in inclusive secondary social studies learning: Direct and indirect learning effects. *Learning Disabilities Research & Practice, 27,* 12–20. doi:10.1111/j.1540-5826.2011.00346.x

Senate Committee on Health, Education, Labor & Pensions. (2017). *Senator Alexander prepared remarks on Congressional Review Act, March 8, 2017.* Retrieved from https://www. help.senate.gov/imo/media/doc/Senator%20Alexander%20prepared%20remarks%20on%20 Accountability%20Congressional%20Review%20Act.pdf

Silver, L.B. (2013). *Changes in DSM-5 and its impact on individuals with learning disabilities.* Retrieved from https://ldaamerica.org/dsm-v-do-the-changes-impact-individuals-with-learning-disabilities/

Smith Lee, S. (2004). Letter to Alice D. Parker, Assistant Superintendent, California Department of Education. Retrieved from https://www2.ed.gov/policy/speced/guid/idea/letters/ 2004-1/parker022004iee1q2004.pdf

Solis, M., Vaughn, S., Swanson E., & McCulley, L. (2012). Collaborative models of instruction: The empirical foundation of inclusion and co-teaching. *Psychology in the Schools, 49,* 498–510. Retrieved from https://eric.ed.gov/?id=EJ989971

Sornson, B. (2015). *Teaching differently in competency-based schools.* Retrieved from https:// www.competencyworks.org/resources/teaching-differently-in-competency-based-schools/

Special Education News. (2017). IDEIA—Individuals with Disabilities Education Improvement Act. Retrieved from http://www.specialednews.com/special-education-dictionary/ ideia---individuals-with-disabilities-education-improvement-act.htm

Stockall, N.S. (2014). When an aide really becomes an aid: Providing professional development for special education paraprofessionals. *Teaching Exceptional Children, 46*(6), 197–205. Retrieved from https://eric.ed.gov/?id=EJ1059282

Strickland, T. & Maccini, P. (2013). The effects of the concrete–representational–abstract integration strategy on the ability of students with learning disabilities to multiply linear expressions within area problems. *Remedial and Special Education, 34*(3), 142–153. doi:10. 1177/0741932512441712

Swanson, E., Solis, M., Ciullo, S., & McKenna, J. (2012). Special education teachers' perceptions and instructional practices in response to intervention implementation. *Learning Disability Quarterly, 35*(2), 115–126. doi:10.1177/0731948711432510

Swanson, H. & Sachse-Lee, C. (2001). A subgroup of analysis of working memory in children with reading disabilities: Domain-general or domain-specific deficiency? *Journal of Learning Disabilities, 34*(3), 249–263. doi:10.1177/002221940103400305

Tannock, R. (2013). Rethinking ADHD and LD in *DSM-5*: Proposed changes in diagnostic criteria. *Journal of Learning Disabilities, 46*(1), 5–25. doi:10.1177/0022219412464341

Teachers College. (n.d.). *Inclusive classrooms project.* Retrieved from http:// inclusiveclassrooms.org/

Tomlinson, C. (2014). *The differentiated classroom: Responding to the needs of all learners* (2nd ed.). Alexandria, VA: ASCD.

Troia, G. & Olinghouse, N. (2013). The common core state standards and evidence-based educational practices: The case of writing. *School Psychology Review, 42*(3), 343–357.

Understood. (2017a). *The difference between IEPs and 504 plans.* Retrieved from https://www.understood.org/en/school-learning/special-services/504-plan/the-difference-between-ieps-and-504-plans

Understood. (2017b). *What to expect at a due process hearing.* Retrieved from https://www.understood.org/en/school-learning/your-childs-rights/dispute-resolution/what-to-expect-at-a-due-process-hearing

United Federation of Teachers. (2016). *Paraprofessionals' responsibilities.* Retrieved from http://www.uft.org/know-your-rights/paraprofessionals-responsibilities

United States Access Board. (n.d.). *Rehabilitation Act of 1973.* Retrieved from https://www.access-board.gov/the-board/laws/rehabilitation-act-of-1973

US Code. (n.d. a). *Elementary and Secondary Education Act of 1965.* Pub. L. 89-10. Retrieved from http://www.scribd.com/doc/49149656/Elementary-and-Secondary-Education-Act-of-1965

US Code. (n.d. b). *Family Educational Rights and Privacy Act (FERPA).* 20 USC. § 1232g. Retrieved from http://uscode.house.gov/view.xhtml?req=granuleid:USC-prelim-title20-section1232g&num=0&edition=prelim

US Courts. (n.d.). *History:* Brown v. Board of Education *re-enactment.* Retrieved from http://www.uscourts.gov/educational-resources/educational-activities/history-brown-v-board-education-re-enactment

US Department of Education. (n.d. a). *Individuals with Disabilities Education Act.* Retrieved from https://sites.ed.gov/idea

US Department of Education. (n.d. b). *Prior written notice.* Retrieved from https://sites.ed.gov/idea/files/modelform2_Prior_Written_Notice.pdf

US Department of Education. (2007). *A guide to the Individualized Education Program.* Retrieved from https://www2.ed.gov/parents/needs/speced/iepguide/index.html

US Department of Education. (2011). *Students with disabilities preparing for postsecondary education: Know your rights and responsibilities.* Retrieved from https://www2.ed.gov/about/offices/list/ocr/transition.html

US Department of Education. (2014). *36th annual report to Congress on the implementation of the Individuals with Disabilities Education Act, 2014.* Washington, DC: US Department of Education, Office of Special Education and Rehabilitative Services, Office of Special Education Programs. Retrieved from https://www2.ed.gov/about/reports/annual/osep/2014/parts-b-c/36th-idea-arc.pdf

US Department of Education. (2015a). *Every Student Succeeds Act.* Retrieved from https://www.ed.gov/essa?src=ft

US Department of Education. (2015b). *FERPA general guidance for parents.* Retrieved from https://www2.ed.gov/policy/gen/guid/fpco/ferpa/parents.html

US Department of Education. (2015c). *Protecting students with disabilities.* Retrieved from https://www2.ed.gov/about/offices/list/ocr/504faq.html

US Department of Education. (2016). *38th annual report to Congress on the implementation of the Individuals with Disabilities Education Act, 2016.* Washington, DC: US Department of Education, Office of Special Education and Rehabilitative Services, Office of Special Education Programs. Retrieved from https://www2.ed.gov/about/reports/annual/osep/2016/parts-b-c/38th-arc-for-idea.pdf

US Department of Education Institute of Education Sciences, National Center for Education Evaluation and Regional Assistance. (2003). *Identifying and implementing educational practices supported by rigorous evidence: A user-friendly guide.* Washington, DC: Coalition for Evidence-Based Policy, Council for Excellence in Government. Retrieved from https://www2.ed.gov/rschstat/research/pubs/rigorousevid/rigorousevid.pdf

US Department of Education Office of Elementary and Secondary Education. (2015). *Public high school 4-year adjusted cohort graduation rate (ACGR), by selected student characteristics and state: 2010–11 through 2014–15.* Retrieved from https://nces.ed.gov/programs/digest/d16/tables/dt16_219.46.asp

US Department of Labor. (n.d. a). *Section 504, Rehabilitation Act of 1973.* 29 USC. § 701. Retrieved from https://www.dol.gov/oasam/regs/statutes/sec504.htm

US Department of Labor. (n.d. b). *Americans with Disabilities Act.* Retrieved from https://www.dol.gov/general/topic/disability/ada

Vanassche, E. & Kelchtermans, G. (2016). A narrative analysis of a teacher educator's professional learning journey. *European Journal of Teacher Education, 39*(3), 355–367. doi:10.1080/02619768.2016.1187127

Vaughn, S. & Wanzek, J. (2014). Intensive interventions in reading for students with reading disabilities meaningful impacts. *Learning Disabilities Research & Practice, 29*(2), 46–53. doi:10.1111/ldrp.12031

Virginia Commonwealth University. (n.d.). *Elementary and Secondary Education Act of 1965.* Retrieved from https://socialwelfare.library.vcu.edu/programs/education/elementary-and-secondary-education-act-of-1965/

Wang, K. (2013). *Between a rock and a hard place: The role of paraprofessionals in special education.* Retrieved from http://www.friendshipcircle.org/blog/2013/11/25/between-a-rock-and-a-hard-place-the-role-of-paraprofessionals-in-special-education/

Watson, S. & Gable, R. (2013). Unraveling the complex nature of mathematics learning disability. Implications for research and practice. *Learning Disability Quarterly, 36*(3), 178–187. doi:10.1177/0731948712461489

Watson, S., Gable, R., Gear, S., & Hughes, K. (2012). Evidence-based strategies for improving the reading comprehension of secondary students: implications for students with LD. *Learning Disabilities Research & Practice, 27*(2), 79–89. doi:10.1111/j.1540-5826.2012.00353.x

Werts, M. & Carpenter, E. (2013). Implementation of tasks in RTI: Perceptions of special education teachers. *Teacher Education and Special Education: The Journal of Teacher Education Division of the Council for Exceptional Children, 36*(3), 246–257. doi:10.1177/0888406413495420

Wright, P.W.D. (2010). *The history of special education.* Retrieved from http://www.wrightslaw.com/law/art/history.spec.ed.law.htm

Young, N.D., Michael, C.M., & Citro, T.A. (2017). *To campus with confidence: Supporting the successful transition to college for students with learning disabilities.* Madison, WI: Atwood.

Zenner, C., Herrnleben-Kurz, S., & Walach, H. (2014). Mindfulness-based interventions in schools—A systematic review and meta-analysis. *Frontiers in Psychology, 5.* doi:10.3389/fpsyg.2014.00603

About the Authors

Dr. **Nicholas D. Young**, PhD, EdD, has worked in diverse educational roles for more than twenty-eight years, serving as a principal, special education director, graduate professor, graduate program director, graduate dean, and longtime superintendent of schools. He was named the Massachusetts Superintendent of the Year, and he completed a distinguished Fulbright program focused on the Japanese educational system through the collegiate level.

Dr. Young is the recipient of numerous other honors and recognitions, including the General Douglas MacArthur Award for distinguished civilian and military leadership and the Vice Admiral John T. Hayward Award for exemplary scholarship. He holds several graduate degrees, including a PhD in educational administration and an EdD in educational psychology.

Dr. Young has served in the US Army and US Army Reserves combined for more than thirty-three years; he graduated with distinction from the US Air War College, the US Army War College, and the US Navy War College. After completing a series of senior leadership assignments in the US Army Reserves as the commanding officer of the 287th Medical Company (DS), the 405th Area Support Company (DS), the 405th Combat Support Hospital, and the 399th Combat Support Hospital, he transitioned to his current military position as a faculty instructor at the US Army War College in Carlisle, Pennsylvania. He currently holds the rank of colonel.

Dr. Young is also a regular presenter at state, national, and international conferences, and he has written many books, book chapters, and articles on various topics in education, counseling, and psychology. Some of his most recent books include *Dog Tags to Diploma: Understanding and Addressing the Educational Needs of Veterans, Servicemembers, and their Families* (in-press); *From Cradle to Classroom: Identifying and Addressing the Educational Needs of Our Youngest Children* (in-press); *Achieving Results: Max-*

imizing Success in the Schoolhouse (in-press); *Emotions and Education: Promoting Positive Mental Health in Students with Learning* (in press); *Paving the Pathway for Educational Success: Effective Classroom Interventions for Students with Learning Disabilities* (in press); *Wrestling with Writing: Effective Strategies for Struggling Students* (in press); *Floundering to Fluent: Reaching and Teaching the Struggling Student* (in press); *From Lecture Hall to Laptop: Opportunities, Challenges, and the Continuing Evolution of Virtual Learning in Higher Education* (2017); *The Power of the Professoriate: Demands, Challenges, and Opportunities in 21st Century Higher Education* (2017); *To Campus with Confidence: Supporting the Successful Transition to College for Students with Learning Disabilities* (2017); *Educational Entrepreneurship: Promoting Public-Private Partnerships for the 21st Century* (2015); *Beyond the Bedtime Story: Promoting Reading Development during the Middle School Years* (2015); *Betwixt and Between: Understanding and Meeting the Social and Emotional Developmental Needs of Students During the Middle School Transition Years* (2014); *Learning Style Perspectives: Impact upon the Classroom* (3rd ed., 2014); *Collapsing Educational Boundaries from Preschool to PhD: Building Bridges across the Educational Spectrum* (2013); *Transforming Special Education Practices: A Primer for School Administrators and Policy Makers* (2012); and *Powerful Partners in Student Success: Schools, Families and Communities* (2012). He has also coauthored several children's books, including the popular series I Am Full of Possibilities. Dr. Young may be contacted directly at nyoung1191@aol.com.

Professor **Kristen Bonanno-Sotiropoulos**, MS, has worked in education at various levels for more than a dozen years. Her professional career within K12 public education included roles as a special education teacher and special education administrator at the elementary and middle school levels. After her tenure in K12, she transitioned to higher education to teach undergraduate and graduate courses as an assistant professor of special education at Springfield College in Springfield, Massachusetts. From there, she moved to Bay Path University as an assistant professor and coordinator of the special education graduate programs. Professor Bonanno-Sotiropoulos received her bachelor of science in liberal studies and elementary education with academic distinction as well as a master of science in moderate disabilities from Bay Path University. She is currently an EdD in educational leadership and supervision candidate at American International College, where she is focusing her research on evidence-based special education practices. She has coauthored a series of book chapters related to the unique needs of struggling readers as well as how higher education institutions can assist special needs students with making a successful transition to college. Her current research interests include, among other areas, effective instructional programs and practices to assist learning disabled students with meeting rigorous academic expectations at all academic levels from preschool to college. Professor Bonnano-Sotiropoulous has become a regular presenter at regional and national conferences and can be reached at kbsotiropoulos@baypath.edu.

Attorney **Jennifer Smolinski** has worked in education for more than three years. Her role within higher education includes the creation and directing of the Center for Disability Services and Academic Accommodations at American International College in Springfield, Massachusetts. She has also taught criminal justice and legal research and writing classes within the field of higher education. Prior to her work at the collegiate level, Attorney Smolinski worked as a solo practitioner conducting education and disability advocacy as well as representing clients in real estate and business matters.

Smolinski received a bachelor of arts in anthropology and a bachelor of arts in sociology from the University of Connecticut, a master's in psychology and counseling as well as a master's of higher education in student affairs from Salem State University, and a law degree from Massachusetts School of Law. She is currently an EdD in educational leadership and supervision candidate at American International College, where she is focusing her research on special education and laws to protect students with disabilities in the classroom.

Smolinski has become a regular presenter educating the faculty, staff, and students at institutes of higher education on disabilities and accommodations at the collegiate level and has presented to local high school special education departments on the transition to college under the Americans with Disabilities Act. She can be reached at Jennifer.Smolinski@aic.edu.